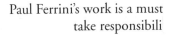 

Paul Ferrini's work is a must
take responsibili

J OHN B RADSHAW

Paul Ferrini's books are the most important I have read.
I study them like a Bible.

E LISABETH K ÜBLER- R OSS

Paul Ferrini's writing will inspire you to greater insights
and understandings, to more clarity and a grander resolve
to make changes in your life that can truly change the world.

N EALE D ONALD W ALSCH

Paul Ferrini is an important teacher in the new millenium.
Reading his work has been a major awakening for me.

I YANLA V ANZANT

Paul Ferrini is a modern day Kahlil Gibran— poet, mystic,
visionary, teller of truth.

L ARRY D OSSEY

I feel that this work comes from a continuous friendship with the
deepest Part of the Self. I trust its wisdom.

C OLEMAN B ARKS

Paul Ferrini reconnects us to the Spirit Within,
to that place where even our deepest wounds can be healed.

J OAN B ORYSENKO

Paul Ferrini's wonderful books show us a way to walk lightly with
joy on planet Earth.

G ERALD J AMPOLSKY

Book Design by Lisa Carta

ISBN # 978-1-879159-96-9

HAVING THE TIME OF YOUR LIFE!

*Working with Cycles
to Realize Your Full Potential*

PAUL FERRINI

TABLE OF CONTENTS

Introduction

The information presented in this book comes from years of experience working with planetary cycles and symbolical systems, and significant time exploring the numerological structure of our base-ten number system and its connection to sacred geometry. The meaning behind the numbers and the geometrical forms they reference permeates every aspect of our lives, although most of us are not conscious of this.

However, this is neither a technical nor a theoretical book. It is a practical book that offers us a tool for understanding where we are in our lives. I have used this work with cycles in my spiritual counseling practice for over 35 years. During this time I have found that it is often stunningly accurate and helps people get a real perspective of where they are in their developmental cycles.

Once they have that understanding, they no longer need to judge, apologize or beat themselves up for how they are living, thinking and feeling. Instead, they can accept what is happening in their lives and turn their focus to where it should appropriately be for the stage that they are in.

Removing judgment, guilt and fear goes a long way in helping us become present to ourselves and others. It is my hope that this book will be a useful tool in your own process and that it will bring you closer to your essential self so that you can live your life authentically and peacefully.

Please be careful not to take this tool and turn it into a weapon to beat up on yourself and others. Don't let the words here become part of an arbitrary authority structure into which you and the people you know must fit. When the fit is there, be grateful for it. When it is not, put the book down and listen to the wisdom that is already there in your heart.

Ideally this book will take you to your heart, not away from it. But that depends, I suppose, on how you use it. If you use these concepts to intellectualize your experience and try to figure everything out, then you will be disappointed. There is no formula that can tie everything up into a nice, neat package.

All nice neat packages will be ripped apart by the tides and tempests of life and their contents strewn about on the oceans of time. No, this book cannot offer you instant organization for the vagaries and incongruities of life. They will remain intact even when everything else falls apart.

The only thing that is certain in life is the uncertainty principle or, as Lao Tzu said, "The only thing that does not change is change itself." So sit back and take all of this with a grain of salt. Sometimes it will pierce the veil with laser-like clarity, and sometimes it will surround you in a fog of words. When the fog comes, anchor in your heart and let the waves lick your boat. You can't see where you are going, so why try to go there. Be patient and wait.

When the fog lifts, clarity and direction will return.

This is not a tool that will always work when and how you want it to. No such tool exists. This tool works best when you approach it humbly and with openness in your heart and mind.

1

PART ONE

Understanding Cycles

GETTING TO KNOW WHO YOU ARE

I t is said that cats have nine lives. What is true for cats may also be true for human beings.

Within the course of our lives, we die and are reborn many times. Of course, I am not talking about physical death, but about psychological death and rebirth.

We are who we think we are. We live out from the internalized beliefs that we have about ourselves or others. Those beliefs about ourselves—the ways we define who we are—are not static. They are constantly changing.

Like a plant, an idea or belief begins as a seed. It is nurtured and it grows. It expresses and extends itself as leaves and flowers. And finally the flowers wither, fall off and seed the ground.

What began as a seed now has returned to seed. A cycle is complete.

This does not just happen once in your life. It happens many times. Who you are now is not who you were ten years ago, or twenty years ago. You have changed.

Of course, some things change and some things do not. Your essence does not change. But your understanding and beliefs change. And, as they change, you live in a different way.

UNDERSTANDING CYCLES

Each cycle is an expression of who you are. Each cycle represents a shift in energy and intention. Each cycle incorporates and integrates what you learned and experienced in the previous cycle.

You are a work in progress. That progress expresses itself in numerous consecutive cycles.

Each time you go through a cycle, you have the opportunity to learn about who you are in a new way and to redefine yourself and your approach to life.

NINE CYCLES OF LIFE

A person who lives to be 81 years old goes through nine consecutive nine year cycles.

The first cycle begins at birth and ends on the 9th birthday. This is the root or archetypal cycle. It is synonymous with childhood.

The second cycle begins at age 9 and ends at the 18th birthday. It is synonymous with adolescence.

The third cycle begins at 18 and ends on the 27th birthday. It is synonymous with early adulthood and with advanced schooling and preparation for making a living and taking responsibility for one's own life.

The fourth cycle begins at 27 and ends on the 36th birthday. It involves building the foundation of career and family.

The fifth cycle begins at 36 and ends on the 45th birthday. During this cycle we begin to experience the shift that comes as we approach our mid-life crisis and we begin to redefine who we are. For some people, changes in career and family structure may occur.

The sixth cycle begins at 45 and ends on the 54th birthday. This is a time when our children leave the nest and our mid life crisis often continues, along with the changes that come with menopause. We begin to realize that we no longer fit into the family structure and communities that have defined us in the last two cycles and we begin the search for new spiritual families and support systems.

The seventh cycle begins at 54 and ends at 63. Often, we become grandparents in this cycle, if we did not in the previous cycle. These are the years when we come fully into our power and purpose and become teachers, leaders and role models for the next generation. Our creative fulfillment and the recognition by others of our talents and gifts (or the lack of fulfillment and recognition) are particularly poignant at this stage of our lives.

The eighth cycle begins at 63 and ends at 72. In this cycle we may experience health issues and crises and we may need to make lifestyle changes that enable us to heal and find greater balance in our lives. We may decide to retire or cut back on the number of hours that we work. We may downsize or relocate to a warmer climate. We may need to get more support from others to continue to live independently.

The ninth cycle begins at 72 and ends at 81. These are our wisdom years when we begin to detach from the world and come to peace with our lives and the people who are closest to us. We may have opportunities to forgive and to heal that were not possible till now because we were not ready. Often we simplify our lives, explore our spirituality and let go of roles/activities that make us anxious or drain our energy. In this last ninth cycle, we also begin thinking about our legacy and preparing to make our transition.

Of course, many people live to be older than 81 and they may experience a 10th or even 11th nine year cycle. However, the readings in this book do not go beyond the ninth year of the ninth cycle (81).

DETERMINING YOUR YEAR

Please keep in mind that your first year of life begins at birth and ends on your first birthday. So at age 1, you are actually beginning your second year of life.

To compute the year that you are in, you always add 1 to your present age.

For example if you are 56 you are in your 57th year. If you are 14, you are in your 15th year.

FINDING OUT WHEN YOUR YEAR BEGINS AND ENDS

The year you are in begins at your last birthday and continues until your next birthday. For example, if you are 56, your 57th year begins at age 56 and continues until you are 57 years old. If you are 14, your 15th year begins at age 14 and continues until you are 15.

DETERMINING WHERE YOU ARE IN THE NINE YEAR CYCLE

To identify the specific year you are in within your current nine year cycle, follow these instructions:

⑨ If you are in your tenth year or older, add the digits of your age together to obtain a number between 1 and 9.

For example, if you are in your fourteenth year, add 1+4 = 5. You are in a five year. If you are in your fifty-seventh year, add 5+7=12 and then add 1+2=3. You are in a three year.

Every year of your life therefore corresponds to a number from 1-9 and exhibits the energetic characteristics of that number.

BECOMING AWARE OF THE THEME
FOR YOUR YEAR

It you are sensitive to cycles, you will notice that the theme for each year begins right around your last birthday. If you are not particularly tuned into your cycles, you may not realize how that theme is manifesting in your life until well into that year.

This is very much an individual phenomenon and you will need to find out through experience what is true for you. As you work with your cycles, it will be clear what your own individual timing is. You can also get an idea of your timing by analyzing the previous cycles in your life.

THE THREE STAGES WITHIN EACH CYCLE

People who are in a 1 or a 2 year are at the beginning of a cycle. This is the Formation Stage. People who are in an 8 or 9 year are at the end of a cycle. This is the Detachment Stage. People who are in years 3-7 are in the middle of their cycle. This is the Action Stage.

While action and outward activity are optimal in the middle of a cycle, the beginning and end of each cycle require a turning inward for vision and reflection.

THE TOTAL LENGTH OF EACH CYCLE

The total time of each cycle is 9 years or 108 months. If we subtract out the 9 months for the zero year (see discussion below), each cycle lasts 8 years and 3 months, or a total of 99 months.

2

PART TWO

The Nine Year Cycle

CHART 1

The Nine Years in a Cycle with Keywords for Each Year

8-9 Letting go/ Detaching

0-1 Birthing/ Beginning

7-8 Balancing/ Healing/Forgiving

1-2 Knowing/Defining

6-7 Expressing/Actualizing

2-3 Relating/Communicating

5-6 Supporting/ Belonging

3-4 Focusing/ Implementing

4-5 Growing/ Expanding

FINDING THE MEANING
OF EACH YEAR IN YOUR CYCLE

The information in Part 2 (below) details the meaning of each of the nine years in a cycle. Once you have computed the number from one to nine that corresponds to your age, read the appropriate section below. That will give you a good idea of the major themes associated with this year of your life. To get additional perspective, read the description of the previous year and the following year so that you get a sense of where you have been and where you are going.

Most of what you need to know will be found in this part of the book. Using the description of the year, along with your intuition about your life, will enable you to fill in the details and connect the dots. It is better for you to do this first before you read the descriptions in Part 3.

0 THE ZERO YEAR

The zero year is the preamble to the cycle. It corresponds to the 9 months in utero (from conception to birth) in which the fetus is nurtured and grows. It represents a time of coalescence, internal growth and gestation. This is the time when the blueprint for life that resides in our genes and chromosomes begins to unfold and our physical body is formed, week by week and month by month. The fetus goes through all the phases of the evolutionary cycle, gradually emerging as a unique, individual human being.

While we generally think our first year in the body begins at birth, an argument can be made that it really begins at conception, or nine months before birth.

In this sense, every new cycle is preceded by a nine month period of gestation, in which the new energy coming in can be protected from the harsh demands of outward existence. Creating a space for meditation, inner listening, and radical self care help us to establish the emotional, psychological and physical safety necessary to bring the new energy into manifestation. Generally speaking, the last nine months of the nine year represent this period of gestation from conception to birth.

PINPOINTING THE ZERO YEARS

Your first zero year begins nine months before birth and ends at birth. Your next zero years begin as follows:

- 9 months before your 9th birthday (8 years, 3 months)
- 9 months before your 18th birthday, (17 years, 3 months)
- 9 months before your 27th birthday (26 years, 3 months)
- 9 months before your 36th birthday (35 years, 3 months)
- 9 months before your 45th birthday (44 years, 3 months)
- 9 months before your 54th birthday (53 years, 3 months)
- 9 months before your 63rd birthday (62 years, 3 months)
- 9 months before your 72nd birthday (71 years, 3 months) etc.

Each zero year is actually the last nine months of your nine year cycle. The first three months of your nine year are a time of completion and radical detachment from the past. The remaining nine months of your nine year are the in-utero time when you are pregnant and carrying energy of the new cycle within, allowing it to gradually take form and get ready to manifest.

The zero year is a time of gestation when your whole life appears to be in limbo. The doors to the outside world close and you are floating again in the amniotic fluid. You know that life must change because you are changing, even if you don't know exactly why or how. This is not a time to be engaged in the affairs of the world. It is a time to go within and get in touch with the parts of you that want to be born in the new cycle that will begin in the next nine months.

The zero year is a pre-birth period. It helps you to establish the emotional, psychological, and physical safety you require to create the needed new structures in your life.

1 THE ONE YEAR

ONE YEARS: The first one year begins at birth and ends on the first birthday (0-1). It repeats every nine years (ages 09-10, 18-19, 27-28, 36-37, 45-46, 54-55, 63-64 and 72-73).

NUMINOUS ONE YEAR: 0-1

KEYWORDS: Birth, beginning, initiation, cultivating a new idea or vision, listening for guidance, brainstorming, taking baby steps and exploring the world, being the mother who nurtures and protects the child until the child can stand on his/her own.

WARNING: This is not a time for active manifestation but for self-nurturing, gentle exploration, and baby steps.

LESSON: I must be true to myself, even when others do not understand or agree with the changes that are happening in me.

THE ONE YEAR is the beginning of the cycle. It is about bringing new energy and opportunity into your life. Like a mother, you have just given birth to a new being who needs your love, nurturing, attention and support. There is going to be a period of time in which the baby is dependent on you. He cannot eat or walk on his own. He cannot change his diapers. He needs constant attention.

The same is true for the new idea or vision of self that you are now bringing forth into the world. It is not ready to stand on its own. It needs nurturing and protection. For a time, you need to become the mommy and take care of the needs of the child. While that child will eventually grow up and lead a separate life, right now she needs you.

Nurturing means not having a lot of expectations or putting a lot of pressure on the child. It means letting the child grow organically. It means listening to the needs of the child and letting her tell you when she is ready to begin to separate, interact more with others and explore the outside world.

Similarly, your new vision or concept of self will need time to evolve. You will need to be with it, identify with it, and support it as it begins to find its voice and its shape. You will need to follow behind as it begins to take its first few baby steps. You will have to protect it from strangers who are harsh or critical.

If you are a good mother in year one, your new energy will be safely and firmly established in the world. However, if you are impatient and expect immediate results, you will put too much pressure on yourself and the new energy and vision of self will be undermined.

Your one year is a time for cultivating a vision of where you want your life to go in the next nine years. Getting in touch with your creative energy is essential in a one year. New—or previously ignored—aspects of self are emerging from within and seeking expression. This is a time for continued self-communion, for investigating new opportunities and beginning to take risks you were unable to take previously. However, those risks have to be taken slowly, gradually and patiently or they will bring way too much stress and anxiety.

In year one, you chart a new course for the next nine years and begin to take the first few baby steps forward. Take your time to be present with yourself and explore the new directions that call to you. This is not a time to pin yourself down, make commitments you cannot keep or take on responsibilities that would burden you or hold you back.

Stay in the present. Explore, play, taste, dream, follow your joy and doors will open. Your path will unfold as you trust yourself.

There is nothing usual about a one year. Like year nine, this is a year of change and transformation. Much of what used to work for you in the previous cycle—your job definition, your relationships, your interests, values and beliefs—has begun to shift. In some significant ways, you are being challenged to cultivate a new way of approaching your life. This may result in changes in where you live, whom you live with, what you do for work and how you live. These changes begin to happen in your nine year and become more and more apparent as you come fully into your one year.

Outer changes may be pronounced or not in a one year. The biggest change is happening within. How you feel about yourself, your life, and your relationships is shifting and you may sense that outer changes eventually need to happen. It is important to take this shift seriously.

Forms that constrict or limit you should have begun to degrade and fall apart in year eight and nine. If you have remained attached to these forms when it is time for them to dissolve or be transformed, you can experience a great deal of frustration, or even pain in your life. When form outlives its usefulness it must be discarded. Old limiting habits created in fear must be relinquished for growth to occur.

Many of us fear change and hold on tenaciously to the past. That causes suffering. During the last two years of your life, you have been asked to let go of fear-based security structures that you no longer need and significantly limit your life and your growth. Hopefully you have been able to do that. If not, please don't hold on any more. Let them go so that you can move on in your life. Bring the new energy in so that your life can shift in a more positive direction.

People who hold on when it is time for change to come may create outer events that force them to change, like an accident or health crisis. Perhaps this has already happened for you. If not, pay attention now to what needs to change or life may do it for you. Shiva, the god of destruction, is very good at freeing us from limited patterns that we are attached to. He shakes the ground and burns the buildings down. Then we have to rise like the Phoenix from the ashes.

Don't wait for the fire to come. Let go now. Give yourself permission to create your life anew. That is what a one year asks from you.

WHAT NOT TO DO IN A ONE YEAR

Don't put pressure on yourself to manifest or to be productive. Take the pressure off. This is a year for nurturing and baby steps, not for outward achievement.

Don't try to pin everything down. That isn't possible now. Instead, explore, play, dream, and nurture the vision.

Don't waste time reliving the past. The old self has gone. The person you used to be has vanished. Someone new is being born within. Find out who that person is.

Don't be too serious or solemn. Find the source of joy inside and begin to live out from that place.

Don't try to be a "responsible" adult. In a one year, you need to be a child.

You need to learn to talk and walk and find your way. You are not ready to take on burdens and responsibilities.

Don't try to please others. You don't know who you are or what you need. Listening to others may cause you to abandon the child when he most needs you.

Don't pretend that you know when you don't. Lighten up on yourself. Just be curious and willing to learn and to explore.

AFFIRMATIONS FOR A ONE YEAR

⊚ Growth happens from the inside out. I am willing to trust the child within to explore the world without pressure to produce or expectation of results.

⊚ I am allowing the child to play, explore, and find his/her joy.

⊚ I am patient with myself and take the time to support the child in taking his/her first few baby steps.

⊚ I am gentle with myself and ask others for the time and space I need to nurture my new direction in life.

⊚ I rely on my spiritual practice to stay centered and to live in the present moment.

2 THE TWO YEAR

TWO YEARS: The first two year begins just after the first birthday and continues until the second birthday. It repeats every 9 years (ages 10-11, 19-20, 28-29, 37-38, 46-47, 55-56, 64-65 and 73-74).

NUMINOUS TWO YEAR: 10-11

KEYWORDS: Learning, study, analysis, information gathering, connecting the dots, finding direction, planning, preparation, obtaining constructive feedback, continuing to trust inner guidance.

WARNING: Over-analysis can lead to paralysis. Stay connected to your intuition to keep yourself balanced and to keep your creative energy engaged.

LESSON: A plan that does not balance heart and mind will not bear fruit.

THE TWO YEAR is about study, planning, preparation, research, training, learning the skills and information you need to begin to refine your vision and articulate it to others. In a two year, you begin to plot your course and study the terrain for your journey. You look at options, analyze alternatives, and incorporate the lessons from the past so that you don't repeat your mistakes. You need to take your vision seriously and start preparing for its eventual implementation. You may seek feedback from others, but please do this carefully, consulting only those whose input will be constructive and respectful. The creative idea/vision is still in its early, formative stages, and negative feedback from others can dampen your spirits or even cause you to give up too soon. Often that means keeping silent about your plans and protecting yourself from harsh and unnecessary criticism. On the other hand, you need to study and consult with others who are more knowledgeable and experienced than you are in order to be properly prepared.

In a two year, you separate the wheat from the chaff. You combine analysis with intuition in order to begin making a plan to move forward. In a two year, you look at both sides of the coin, compare one side to the other, role play different possibilities, play devil's advocate, consider all the possibilities, accept and respect different approaches and perspectives as you gradually find what works for you.

The two year is about finding a clear direction. In order to move the energy out into the world, the vision or goal must be clear and the pathway to reach it must be plotted. As you begin to follow the course you have charted, the direction may need to be changed or refined. Obstacles will arrive and you will have to avoid them or push through them. The timetable you expected may not be realistic. You may have to slow down and adjust to the conditions at hand.

There may be times when you need to recognize that you are not adequately prepared for the journey ahead. You may need more knowledge, more experience, and more feedback from people who have expertise. You need to take the time to learn, to fill in the gaps, to deal with challenges or anticipate the obstacles that might arise.

Test the waters before you launch the boat. Build a model before you break ground. Consider and evaluate options and alternatives. Look at things from different perspectives. The more you know before you take action, the more likely you will be to succeed. Remember, a two year is about getting clarity and direction. It is about preparing for the journey. You may not actually take the journey before your three year, but you will be ready when the time to act is near.

WHAT NOT TO DO IN A TWO YEAR

Don't be in a hurry to act or to manifest. It is not time for that. This is a time to gather information and to achieve mental clarity.

Don't seek approval or validation from others. Guard your vision against criticism from others who do not understand. Instead, seek meaningful feedback from those who can support your vision and have more knowledge or experience than you.

Don't try to teach or preach. Be content to be a learner. You have a lot to learn.

Don't be afraid to experiment and try different approaches. Use your mind to evaluate the results. Use your heart to find out what feels right to you.

Don't put a lot of pressure on yourself. This is not a time for "doing" or going into production. That will come later.

On the other hand, don't get lost in daydreaming. This is a time to understand how the dream can become reality.

Don't be lazy. Do your homework. Go to school. Actively prepare so that you are ready to act when the time for action has come.

AFFIRMATIONS FOR A TWO YEAR

☺ I am taking the time to refine my vision and to understand what is necessary for it to become manifest.

☺ I understand that this is not a time to act, but a time to prepare for action.

☺ I am content to be a learner and I am willing to take the time and invest the energy in gathering the information/ obtaining the skills I need.

☺ I know my primary purpose this year is to achieve clarity and find a direction.

☺ In order to do this, I refrain from putting pressure on myself or having huge expectations of imminent success.

☺ I am patient with myself and where I am in the creative process.

☺ I use my mind to analyze the options and opportunities available to me. I use my heart and my intuition to tune into the choices that feel congruent with who I am.

3 THE THREE YEAR

THREE YEARS: The first three year begins just after the second birthday and continues until the third birthday. It repeats every 9 years (ages 11-12, 20-21, 29-30, 38-39, 47-48, 56-57, 65-66 and 74-75).

NUMINOUS THREE YEAR: 20-21

KEYWORDS: Relationship, synthesis, communication, sharing, networking, cooperation, giving and receiving support, accepting differences, learning from others, compromise, conflict-resolution.

WARNING: Relationships must be between equals who appreciate and respect each other if there is going to be mutual support and creative synthesis.

LESSON: The other person's needs and wants are as important as my own.

THE THREE YEAR is about synthesizing different perspectives and beginning to move forward into action. This is the first year in which you are beginning to actively implement your vision and carry it forth into the world. In the process, the vision will need to be tweaked to anticipate the needs and desires of others.

In a three year you are actively making relationships and

building alliances that will help you move forward. Good communication skills and the ability and willingness to interact with a wide variety of people are essential. A three year is very much about networking, spreading the world, letting people know who you are and what you have to offer.

Do not be afraid to tell the truth about your goals, but be open to the ideas of others, as they may help you see things from a new and helpful perspective. So far you have been moving from the inside out in a creative process that solidifies the vision. Now, it may be helpful to see things from the outside, the way others might see them. Whatever you are offering to the world must be relevant and attractive to others. This is the time to be clear about the benefits others will receive from what you offer.

A three year often results in an important new relationship entering your life. That person (or these people) may collaborate with you personally or professionally and help to shape the direction of your life to come. While this is exciting and synchronous, it can also be challenging as you both encounter differences and experience conflicts. Living and/or working with another person requires you to accept and respect the other person's ideas and experiences. You may have to adjust to that person's idiosyncrasies, including differences in communication style, values and life rhythms. At the same time, they must adjust to you or a creative synthesis cannot be made.

Relationships offer you the possibility to grow as a person, to be honest with others, to learn to communicate clearly, to set healthy boundaries, and to give and receive support mentally, emotionally and spiritually. Exploring this treasure trove of relationship helps us learn to have compassion for ourselves and others and to understand what it means to be a human being.

However, it is important for us to realize that most of us have not learned how to love ourselves and be clear about what we want. Often, we project our unworthiness onto others, making judgments about them and getting triggered by the judgments they make about us. Mutual projection and poor communication skills often derail our relationships and bring us more pain than joy.

In order to build healthy relationships with others, we have to be willing to learn how to love ourselves and see our patterns of self-betrayal. That way we can take the blame and shame out of our relationships and we can learn to take responsibility for our own thoughts, feelings, words and actions.

Needless to say, this takes courage and willingness on our part and on the part of our partners, children, and co-workers. Relationships are a crucible. The False Self must die in order for the True Self to be born in each of us. Commitment to becoming true to ourselves and giving others the space to do the same is crucial.

To the extent that a three year brings new relationships into your life, you can be sure that many emotional challenges will arise. There will be opportunities to understand and to heal, to forgive and to tell the truth. If you are up for that, this can be a powerful year of psychological and spiritual growth. If you are not, it can be a difficult and painful year.

The upside of the three year is that it brings new energy and support into your life. The downside is that personality conflicts and poor communication can sabotage your relationship and prevent the new energy from expressing in a way that benefits both people.

WHAT NOT TO DO IN A THREE YEAR

Do not isolate. Reach out and connect with others. Network, interact, dialog, and build new relationships and alliances.

Don't try to do it all by yourself. This is a time for cooperation and collaboration.

Don't insist on having your way all the time. You need to learn to listen to and value the needs and opinions of others.

Don't lie or tell people what you think they want to hear. Communicate honestly and openly so that people know where you are coming from.

Don't put people off or evade commitment. Give your relationships the time and the energy they deserve.

Don't allow conflict to destroy the relationship. Resolve conflicts when they arise and try to understand and accept the other person's ideas and experiences, even when they differ from your own.

Don't project onto others. Take responsibility for your thoughts, feelings, words and actions.

AFFIRMATIONS FOR A THREE YEAR

◎ I am actively communicating my vision to others.

◎ I am reaching out and making new connections.

◎ I am being authentic and allowing myself to be seen and heard.

◎ I am listening to others and accepting what is real and true for them.

◎ I am willing to cooperate. I am willing to negotiate.

◎ I am improving my communication skills.

◎ I am giving my relationship(s) priority time.

◎ I am honest and trustworthy.

◎ I am moving beyond selfishness and limited personal agendas to find areas where I can share and collaborate with others.

THE FOUR YEAR

FOUR YEARS: The first four year begins just after the third birthday and continues until the fourth birthday. It repeats every 9 years (ages 12-13, 21-22, 30-31, 39-40, 48-49, 57-58, 66-67 and 75-76).

NUMINOUS FOUR YEAR: 30-31

KEYWORDS: Practical accomplishment, focused work, building the foundation or structure of life, being grounded, taking responsibility, making commitments, showing up every day, moving toward your goal, implementing your vision.

WARNING: Your dreams cannot become a reality unless you learn to show up for your life every day.

LESSON: There are no more excuses. It is time for me to show up and do my part.

THE FOUR YEAR is about the active implementation of your vision. It is about taking practical, concrete steps to manifest the idea or vision in the world. It is about finding a form that focuses the new energy. It may mean moving into production on a product or a service.

In a four year, you build a structure for your life. You put down roots and build or buy a home or a business. You commit to a relationship or to having a family. You take on

41

responsibilities not because you have to, but because you want to and because taking responsibility helps you to move toward your goal.

In a four year, your commitment becomes concrete and palpable. You learn to show up every day for the job or the relationship. You work hard and feel good about what you are able to achieve. Because of that you eventually succeed, even though there may be challenges or setbacks on the way.

Even those who are most successful in life have had times when they have failed to manifest their dreams. But what sets them apart from others is the fact that they did not give up when they failed. They learned from their mistakes. They reinvented the vision and tried again.

This is a year when you will be focusing on meeting the physical challenges of life: the health and well being of your body, your business, your relationships, and your family. There is nothing esoteric or whimsical about a four year. It is a year of intense, practical work and daily routines help you stay focused and in a good rhythm.

Take the time to eat well, sleep well, get exercise, and care for your body so that it can perform all the tasks you are asking it to do without getting exhausted. Conserve your energy so it is there when you need it.

Being productive requires that you live a balanced and disciplined life both physically and emotionally. You need to avoid lots of ups and downs that create stress and anxiety. Be moderate in what you say and do. Don't bite off more than you can chew. Don't waste your time on distractions that squander your energy. Stay focused on what is important.

Leading a disciplined life will enable you to be productive and realize your goals. You will have the satisfaction of seeing the creative process bear fruit in your life. That will build your self-confidence and reinforce your belief that you can do anything that you set your heart and mind to.

Four years are good years for making decisions and commitments regarding work, career, relationships and family life. They are years when you are stabilizing your life.

WHAT NOT TO DO IN A FOUR YEAR

Do not remain idle. Do not day dream or be lazy. This is a year for action.

Don't over-think or over-plan. Jump into the river and start swimming.

Do not try to be perfect. If you need to be perfect you will never get anything done.

Do not procrastinate. If you are scared, take baby steps toward your goal. Build your confidence with small successes.

Do not make excuses. It you don't believe you can do it you won't. It isn't anyone else's fault or responsibility.

Don't sweat the small stuff. Keep your eyes on the prize.

Don't dwell on your mistakes. Learn from them and avoid making the same mistake in the future.

Don't be hard on yourself or others. Practice forgiving yourself and them too.

Don't give up just because you have a bad day or a bad week. If something doesn't work, try something different. Don't be rigid or headstrong. Adjust to the reality at hand.

AFFIRMATIONS FOR A FOUR YEAR

◎ I am actively communicating my vision to others.

◎ I am actively manifesting my vision.

◎ I take small steps at first until I get confident in what I am doing. Then I gradually take bigger steps.

◎ I focus on one thing at a time, so that I do not get overwhelmed by all the tasks I need to accomplish

◎ I pace myself so that I don't rush, burn out and crash.

◎ I see obstacles as challenges to overcome.

◎ I do not give up when things get difficult. I persevere. I persist. I keep showing up.

◎ I do my best and I know that it will be enough, even if things don't show up the way I want them to.

◎ I do whatever needs to be done. I am willing to get my hands dirty. I refuse to be a prima donna.

◎ I forgive myself and learn from my mistakes.

5

THE FIVE YEAR

FIVE YEARS: The first five year begins just after the fourth birthday and continues until the fifth birthday. It repeats every 9 years (ages 13-14, 22-23, 31-32, 40-41, 49-50, 58-59, 67-68 and 76-77).

NUMINOUS FIVE YEAR: 40-41

KEYWORDS: Expanding consciousness, living outside of the box, psychological growth, self improvement, aspiring to greater understanding, taking risks, traveling to different countries and cultures, transcending false or limited beliefs, being authentic/unique, exploring your talents and gifts, pursuing educational goals, being free to explore life purpose, meaning, and spirituality.

WARNING: Don't let your fears limit you. Don't sell yourself short. Don't settle for less than you aspire to.

LESSON: I have to take risks and move through my fears if I am going to avoid stagnation and learn to think and live outside of the box.

THE FIVE YEAR is about growth, expansion of consciousness, individuation, creative expression, unconventional thinking, travel, taking risks, experimentation, living outside of the box, expanding the form or structure of your life so that growth can occur.

Whereas your previous four year was about creating a form that would consolidate, contain and shape your energy, this year is very different. The five year asks you to grow beyond the structure you created last year. If you do not take the time to explore new directions and expand the form, then you will feel constrained and limited by it. You will live inside a prison of your own making.

The five year reminds you that you have the key to the prison door and you can walk out into the light whenever you are ready. Readiness of course is the key. We are all limited by our fears and negative thinking. We all get stuck in the rut of past patterns. We all dig ourselves in and then have trouble extricating ourselves from dysfunctional patterns.

In a five year, you are challenged to break free, to take risks, to explore new ways of thinking and being. You capacity to do this has a lot to do with how successful your current nine year cycle will be.

The five year is the mid-point of your nine year cycle. In years 1-4, you learned to nurture, communicate, and manifest your creative vision. You brought an idea into the world and anchored it in physical reality. That is all appropriate and helpful. But ideas cannot remain static or they die out.

They must grow and expand. As the content grows the form must expand to contain it. As you grow and individuate as a human being the structure of your life must change to accommodate who you are becoming. Think of it this way. When you are a baby you wear baby clothes. But then your body grows and the baby clothes don't fit any more. So you have to get bigger clothes. What is true for your body is also true for your mind and emotions. As you grow psychologically, you need new and expanded ideas, feelings and experiences. The old ones don't work any more.

Five is a growth year, so don't get stuck in old patterns. Don't rely on old ideas and behaviors. Routines and structures were helpful last year, but they will be limiting this year. Expand your consciousness, travel to a new place, take a class or go back to school, go on a spiritual retreat. Do something that challenges you and brings new energy, understanding and experience into your life.

If you take the time for self expansion and improvement you will know how the structure of your life needs to change to accommodate your ongoing creativity and growth. Don't let your creative projects go dead in the water. Cross the water to a different shore and when you return you will see them differently. You will breathe new life into the old form.

As your consciousness expands, you will better understand who you are and how you can authentically interface with the world around you. You will tune into what others need and what you are able to joyfully and enthusiastically give.

The five year is about spiritual renewal. It is a time for YOU to grow and change. If you take the time to do that, you return to the world as a change agent. You better understand your life purpose and direction. You know more accurately where and how to invest your energies. Taking time for yourself away from the world and the familiar structures of your life helps you to better understand how to be in the world as an authentic person.

When Jesus told us that our challenge was to be "in the

world" but not "of the world," he was cautioning us not to allow the needs of others to define us. Instead, we must know and define ourselves so that we can respond honestly to others and find ways to share our talents and gifts with those who need them. Of course, this is a lifetime process. It is not limited just to this year of your life. But in this year it is of primary importance. This is a transitional year. Use this time well and you will come into your power and purpose in this cycle. The energy of the cycle will be renewed and sustained. Years six and seven will bring greater visibility and success. You will surpass limits and gain a new and more rooted confidence in yourself.

WHAT NOT TO DO IN A FIVE YEAR

Don't try to see the forest through the trees. Find the road out of the forest.

Don't limit yourself. Don't get stuck in your mundane patterns and routines.

Don't be defined by what you do. Let who you are define what you do.

Don't be rigid or allow your life to become boring and predictable.

Be open to change.

Don't let your fear and your need for security run your life. Take some risks.

Don't settle for less than you aspire to.

AFFIRMATIONS FOR A FIVE YEAR

- I am taking time to expand my consciousness.

- I am willing to learn to live and think outside of the box.

- I am willing to take some risks and have new growth experiences.

- I am willing to let the structure of my life be more flexible so that I am less limited by it.

- I am willing to make time for my spiritual growth and well being.

- I am pursuing my educational or self improvement goals.

- I am learning to see the big picture instead of getting lost in the details.

- I am exploring my unique talents and gifts.

6 THE SIX YEAR

SIX YEARS: The first six year begins just after the fifth birthday and continues until the sixth birthday. It repeats every 9 years (ages 14-15, 23-24, 32-33, 41-42, 50-51, 59-60, 68-69 and 77-78).

NUMINOUS SIX YEAR: 50-51

KEYWORDS: Social connections and support, nuclear and extended family, communities, compassion, service to others, the need to belong and be accepted, public approval, social image or mask, appearances, social graces/manners, cults or cliques, conformity to norms, modeling health, beauty and harmony, publicity, advertising, marketing, social media.

WARNING: Seek community with others but don't let your need for social approval cause you to conform to norms and values that you do not share.

LESSON: I need to look beyond appearances and see the person behind the mask.

THE SIX YEAR is about joining in community with other people who share your values, beliefs and interests. This includes being part of a nuclear family and an extended family or spiritual community.

Whereas year five had a lot to do with exploring, reinforcing and refining your personal beliefs, year six is devoted to finding support and confirmation for those beliefs in a group of people. Like most people, you want to belong to something greater than yourself. You want to bond and have a shared experience with others.

Unfortunately, people sometimes bond in a way that excludes others and make the members of the group feel privileged or special. This can result in social norms that are rigid or harsh, as they are in many cults and some religious or political groups. These groups play upon the fears of their members and pump them up by condemning others or seeing others as less wise or less worthy. Often, these groups have a charismatic leader to whom people give away their power and often their money.

So the negative expression of the search for social connection is about conformity to group norms at the expense of one's personal freedom. Indeed, in some groups, leaving is not an option, or the price one pays for leaving is social ostracism and public humiliation. In these groups, it is a "sin" to be different. Following the beat of your own drum is not possible.

On the other hand, positive bonding and social fulfillment happens in groups that are inclusive rather than exclusive. In these groups, you may buy into the norms but you also feel free to disagree with others and to be yourself.

When groups respect the right of individual members to have their own ideas and experiences, people are able to meet their need for belonging without sacrificing their uniqueness or their freedom.

Of course, everyone is different in terms of what he or she needs in a group experience, but the struggle in a six year is always about the tension between freedom vs. conformity. Some people have a stronger need for belonging than for freedom. Others cannot belong to a group unless they feel free to be themselves. Where do you stand? What is your experience?

Another aspect of six is the tendency to see people only through their social mask/public image or the roles that they play. Seeing only the appearance, not the substance, can be misleading. It is all too possible to judge the book by its cover and make superficial judgments about others that are untrue and uncharitable.

The six year is a year lived in the public domain. You are visible in your community. People know you at least superficially. That gives you a sense of place and a context for being.

Another aspect of six is compassion and service to others. Often, in spiritual or political groups, there are opportunities to volunteer to help others who are less fortunate. The great epiphany you experience in a six year is, as John Donne wrote, "No man is an island." You do not live for yourself alone, but also for the survival, dignity and well being of others.

Rabbi Hillel asked "If I am for myself alone, who am I?" If our life does not include and benefit others, then it is not a generous or a spiritual life. But Hillel also asked "If I am not for myself, who is for me?" One does not live a spiritual life by ignoring one's own needs for individuation.

Finding a balance between the needs of the individual (symbolized by the number 5) and the needs of the group (symbolized by the number 6) is one of the ongoing challenges of life. The art is to cultivate self knowledge and fidelity to self while reaching out to share with others and serve our fellow human beings with understanding and compassion.

The number six underscores and highlights your need for social acceptance. You may try to please others in order to gain their approval. You want people to like you and you learn to show up in the ways they want or expect you to, even though it might not be honest or authentic. Wearing a mask to gain social approval is one of the ways in which you can betray yourself. You may be successful in getting noticed and appreciated, but you give others a false idea of who you are. While you might be able "to fake it" for a while, in the end you cannot show up as someone you are not. When you can no longer show up as people expect, they are disappointed and may even feel betrayed by you.

In this sense you need to be careful about the masks you wear and the promises you make. If you seduce others or make promises you cannot keep, you will earn their wrath, not their praise.

Because the number six has a lot to do with public acceptance and approval it also reflects who you choose as your role models—the leaders, singers, movie stars, sports heroes, etc. that you admire and want to be like.

Much of the health, entertainment and glamour industry is built on our collective need to look and be like others. We spend a lot of money on diets and weight loss programs, cosmetic surgery, and a variety of programs and products that promise to help us look or feel better so that we can fit in, be noticed and get the attention and approval we all crave.

The desire to have health, beauty and harmony in our lives is all part of the domain of the number six. And a six year often involves some effort on your part to improve your image in the attempt to be noticed and attract others.

Marriage and family are also an important part of the domain of the number six. The family is the primary social unit of our society. In our families we learn to nurture and support others. We often sacrifice or postpone our own needs and desires to help our partners or our children grow and thrive. In this sense, our families are the building blocks of the social network that we create in our lives, learning to share with and serve others in the larger communities where we live.

A six year is a good year for public ceremonies like weddings, family gatherings, community events, fund raisers, etc. In a six year, you put your best foot forward and your image is on the line. Because you are seen by the public, you will receive your share of praise and criticism and you need to have the inner strength and integrity to handle both.

WHAT NOT TO DO IN A SIX YEAR

Don't isolate. Cultivate your connections with your family, extended family, your church or spiritual group, and other groups where you feel safe and accepted.

Don't get seduced by cults/cliques with high exclusivity and rigid norms that limit your freedom to be and express yourself.

Don't get mesmerized by appearances. Look more deeply. See the person behind the role or mask.

Don't be dishonest or inauthentic in the attempt to gain the attention and approval of others.

Do not try to please others in ways that are not congruent with who you are.

Don't be seductive or insincere. Don't make promises you cannot keep.

Don't be self-centered. Find opportunities to serve others who are less fortunate.

Don't play small or hold yourself back. Let yourself be seen and heard.

Don't be afraid to follow the lead of people you admire and respect. But also be willing to play a leadership role if this comes naturally.

Don't be too solemn or serious. Take time to have fun and to experience beauty and harmony in all its forms.

AFFIRMATIONS FOR A SIX YEAR

⊚ I am reaching out to others and finding groups where I feel safe and my needs for connection and belonging are met.

⊚ I am seeking groups that are inclusive, not exclusive.

⊚ I am looking beyond appearances.

⊚ I am aware that my attempt to please others in order to win their approval may lead to self-betrayal and/or betrayal of others.

⊚ I want to be with people who share my interests and values without judging or condemning others who are different.

🌀 I am caring for my family.

🌀 I am becoming more active in my community.

🌀 I am willing to be seen, heard, and known by others.

🌀 I am cultivating compassion and taking advantage of opportunities to help and to serve.

7 THE SEVEN YEAR

SEVEN YEARS: The first seven year begins just after the sixth birthday and continues until the seventh birthday. It repeats every 9 years (ages 15-16, 24-25, 33-34, 42-43, 51-52, 60-61, 69-70 and 78-79).

NUMINOUS SEVEN YEAR: 60-61

KEYWORDS: Success, active and authentic creative expression, achievement, leadership, mastery, performing, teaching, sharing confidently and widely with others, motivating and inspiring others, abundance, prosperity, trust, spontaneity, grace, receiving attention and praise, public notoriety or fame.

WARNING: You cannot achieve the recognition that you crave without confidence in yourself and trust in your creative process.

LESSON: It is time to confront the insecurity and unworthiness that fuel my narcissism, perfectionism and need to control.

THE SEVEN YEAR: Years 3-7 are the active years in your cycle. With hard work in year four, exploration of meaning and purpose in year five, and public participation in community in year six, you have laid the groundwork for success. Your seven year thus brings fruition and achievement of all that you have worked for.

The seven year is about achievement and mastery. It is the year when you shine and people are inspired by your example. This happens naturally when you have confidence in yourself, when you trust your creative process and take advantage of the opportunities for self-expression that spontaneously arise in your life.

On the other hand, if you lack self-confidence, don't trust the process, and don't walk through the open doors in your life, you may experience great frustration and unhappiness. You may feel that success eludes you and people don't understand or appreciate who you are or what you have to offer.

However, if you are honest with yourself, you know that this is not someone else's issue. It is yours. You are the one who is blocking your own success.

People who struggle in year seven come into it with a big ego agenda and rigid pictures of the way their work is to be offered and received. They frequently exhibit perfectionist thinking and behavior, turning down opportunities that could give them visibility because they are not glamorous enough or do not pay a high enough honorarium. They try to control what happens and this shuts down the creative process and aborts the spontaneous flow of energy from the inside out.

Another way of saying this is they do not follow their hearts but live in their heads trying to figure everything out. They often have a superiority complex, thinking that they are more talented than others. However, this "superiority" masks the fact that they feel "less than others" and unconfident inside.

Their lack of self worth and emotional neediness—which they compensate for by a narcissistic approach (*It's all about me.*)—turn other people off. As a result, they do not get the praise and validation from others that they so desperately crave. Sometimes they may experience public criticism or even humiliation.

All of this would turn around if they could love and affirm themselves and share with others authentically without putting a lot of pressure on themselves to "perform" or on others to respond to their performance. By taking baby steps they would build self confidence and begin to trust their own creative process.

Perfectionism and egotism are the death knell of the creative process. The need to control actually creates what they fear the most: rejection and disapproval. They also live in a vicious cycle of victimhood, lack and poverty consciousness. Because they do not value themselves and trust the universe to support them they shut down the flow of abundance and continue to create a reality in which they do not have enough money or resources to thrive. Because they don't feel as if they are enough, they never have enough.

The number seven in its natural flow spontaneously leads to abundance. When you trust in who you are and share easily and authentically with others, people tend to respond to you positively, even enthusiastically. You are guided to the right audience and the venues for your work even if they are not large or glamorous. Because you keep your expectations modest and feel gratitude for any opportunity to share, you take small concrete steps toward your goal and build self-confidence. In this way the audience for your work can steadily and organically grow. Little successes lead to larger ones.

That is what it takes to lead a life of success and abundance. Your creative energy naturally flows from self to others and you feel supported by the universe in your self expression. The more joy and gratitude you feel for each opportunity to touch others, the more palpable that universal support feels to you. Indeed, your life begins to feel like a dance or partnership with the divine.

In year seven, people look to you as a teacher, a leader, a guide. You model for them the kind of joyful success that they too can achieve in their lives. Since your cup is full it is natural to allow its contents to flow out to others. By witnessing your trust in the universe they learn to stop trying to control their own creative process. They learn to put down their ego agendas and get out of their own way so that their talents and gifts can be expressed.

The number seven is about expressing your talents and gifts and helping others learn to do the same. This is an empowerment process. As a master, you model for others what they can do. You do not puff yourself up or make yourself special. There is no specialness in the universe. Everyone is worthy of love and has something to give.

For some folks, the seven year challenges them to understand what did not work so that they can learn from their mistakes, make corrections in their controlling, perfectionist approach, practice self forgiveness, and work on the core self-esteem issues that are necessary for creative success.

Those who have overbearing egos and are filled with hubris may have to be knocked down a peg or two so that they can learn humility. Self-centeredness and grandiosity rarely lead to a convivial life where our gifts and those of others can be easily given and received.

WHAT NOT TO DO IN A SEVEN YEAR

Don't have rigid expectations of how your creative process will be received by others. Let go of your pictures of the way you think things should look and trust the process.

Don't be a perfectionist. Take advantage of the opportunities that spontaneously arise even though they may not feed your ego.

Don't close the door. If it opens it means you are supposed to walk through it.

Don't seek validation from others. Share because it is joyful and you love to do it.

Don't put pressure on yourself to perform or others to respond to you.

Don't be a prima donna. You are not more important than others.

Don't be a victim. Don't feel sorry for yourself. If people aren't appreciating you or your gifts, it means you are needy, have self-esteem issues and have not learned to love and value yourself.

Don't live in lack and poverty consciousness. The universe will support you when you trust the process and learn to live in gratitude.

AFFIRMATIONS FOR A SEVEN YEAR

⊚ I trust my creative process and say yes to the opportunities that arise to share authentically with others.

⊚ I surrender my expectations and show up with an open heart.

⊚ I trust my talents and gifts and express them joyfully.

⊚ I share as an equal not as someone who is special.

⊚ I am not afraid to shine.

⊚ When I shine, I inspire, uplift and empower others.

⊚ I give freely without strings attached or thought of return.

⊚ I trust that when I do my best the universe will support me.

⊚ I live in gratitude.

⊚ I live in abundance and know there is enough for all of us.

8 THE EIGHT YEAR

EIGHT YEARS: The first eight year begins just after the seventh birthday and continues until the eighth birthday. It repeats every 9 years (ages 16-17, 25-26, 34-35, 43-44, 52-53, 61-62, 70-71 and 79-80).

NUMINOUS EIGHT YEAR: 70-71

KEYWORDS: Psychological adjustment, lessons learned, correction, healing, forgiveness, shift in energy from outward to inward, time to rest, recharge, find more balance, pain as a wake up call, psychological death and rebirth, coming to peace and reconciliation.

WARNING: You will find yourself in the throes of a healing crisis if you do not heed the message that pain has brought to you.

LESSON: It is time for me to heal, forgive and see how my life is out of balance.

THE EIGHT YEAR: After seven years, the active phase of the cycle has come to an end and in your eighth year your energy shifts direction and begins to move inward. You take time to reflect on what you have accomplished and to get perspective. You come to grips with any mistakes you have made and do your best to learn from them. You see how you could have done things differently and had more success and fewer struggles. Yet you also recognize that you did what you could do with the consciousness that you had at the time and you forgive yourself and others. Gradually you accept the lessons that have come to you in the active phase of this cycle and you become reconciled to the results you have achieved.

Having expressed yourself actively in the world, you understand now that it is time to rest and to recharge. Your cup has been emptied and now needs to be filled again with a new awareness and energy.

An eight year is often a time when you experience some kind of healing crisis. Things need to shift inside of you so that your energy can be restored and you can come into greater balance. Taking the time to heal and adjust is an important part of the eight year. Having given a lot of yourself to others, it now becomes necessary to allow yourself to receive the care and nurturing you need.

As you reflect on your accomplishments and challenges you may find it helpful to have the support of a mentor or therapist who can sit with you, listen deeply and help you forgive and come to peace with yourself and others. It is also a wonderful time to attend a spiritual retreat or be actively engaged in a spiritual practice.

During your eight year, you take the time to integrate your experience into the warp and woof of your life. Your outward activity slows down so that you can have time to internalize what you have learned. This is a process that requires patience. Pressure to act, decide, or move outward with your energy is counterproductive and will impede the internalization process.

Some of us have difficulty slowing down and taking time for ourselves. To help us, our soul may create some kind of illness, accident or other life-changing event that prevents us from being engaged in the world and forces us to rest and look within ourselves. While that event might initially seem tragic or be life-threatening, in retrospect we can see how it was necessary to get our attention and to help us re-focus our lives.

The themes of psychological death and rebirth are an essential part of the number eight. If the old patterns of thinking and acting are not voluntarily relinquished, if the need for healing is not recognized, then change may come from the outside. This is sometimes a painful way to learn but pain does get our attention. Pain is a wake-up call that tells us that we are out of balance and that something inside of us needs to shift.

Your eight year is successful when you are able to consciously accept your need for healing and re-balancing and when you take the time to go within and make the psychological adjustments that are necessary for your health and well-being. Being humble and asking for the help of experienced healing practitioners can make a big difference in your success.

This is not a time when you have to do it all alone. Help is available and nurturing and support are what you need. On the other hand, no one else is going to wave a magic wand and heal you. Healing happens from the inside out when you are ready and willing. Others can assist you in the healing process, but they cannot do it for you.

Healing and reconciliation in your eighth year make it far easier to let go of the past in year nine when you are asked to detach and get ready to receive the energy of the new cycle.

WHAT NOT TO DO IN AN EIGHT YEAR

Don't try to stay actively engaged in the world. This is a time when the direction of your energy needs to shift and move inward.

Don't rush out like Don Quixote to fight the windmills and save the damsels in distress. Come back home and heal your wounds.

Don't try to medicate or escape from your pain. Pain is a messenger that needs to be heard.

Don't ignore your healing crisis. Take time to rest, rebalance and refocus your life.

Don't resist the lessons your life has brought to you. It is time to accept your mistakes and learn from them.

Don't try to pick up the pieces of your life and put Humpty Dumpty back on the wall. Let the old life die so that a new life can be born

Don't insist on healing by yourself. Find the help you need.

Don't blame yourself or others. Practice forgiveness and find peace and reconciliation.

AFFIRMATIONS FOR AN EIGHT YEAR

⊚ I am willing to slow down, step back and take time for understanding and reflection.

⊚ I am taking the time to internalize what has happened and what I have learned during the last seven years.

⊚ I am facing the lessons life brings.

⊚ I am feeling my pain and heeding the message it brings.

⊚ I am opening up to the shift that needs to happen within me in order for me to create a more balanced life.

⊚ I am open to finding help from skilled healing practitioners.

⊚ I am reconciled to the past and ready to let go of it.

⊚ I am committed to my spiritual practice.

9

THE NINE YEAR

NINE YEARS: The first nine year begins just after the eighth birthday and continues until the ninth birthday. It repeats every 9 years (ages 17-18, 26-27, 35-36, 44-45, 53-54, 62-63, 71-72 and 80-81).

NUMINOUS NINE YEAR: 80-81

KEYWORDS: Completion, detachment, letting go, withdrawing from the affairs of the world, entering the inner temple, moving into the state of chrysalis, the womb or in utero experience, getting ready to be born again. The last nine months of this year comprise the zero year.

WARNING: If you do not detach and let go, you will hold onto the past and new energy will not be able to come into your life.

LESSON: I did the best I could with the consciousness I had. No regrets. I need to accept what happened, forgive myself and let go.

THE NINE YEAR is about completion, detachment and letting go. Ongoing forgiveness practice helps you to relinquish the past and move into a state of silence in which thinking and action slow down. In a nine year, you come to peace with all that has happened in your cycle and wipe the slate clean so that you are ready for new experiences in your one year.

Outward activity and focus are inappropriate for a nine year. Many people going into a nine year do not understand why they lack the motivation to do anything. They do not want to appear to others as lazy or irresponsible so they often try to remain active in the affairs of the world when they have little energy to do so. They spin their wheels, expending a lot of energy going nowhere and they can become very frustrated.

Don't let that happen to you. Understand that this is not a time when you should be making new commitments or engaging in outward activity. You are like a bear hibernating for the winter, turning inward to reconcile yourself with the past and regenerate your energy.

Energy in a nine year is pulled in, contained, sealed off from the distractions of the world. Of course, you may be afraid that this state of limbo will last forever and that you will never emerge from your cave and reenter the world. However, when you understand your cycles, you learn to be patient and wait, knowing that the time of rebirth will come when you are ready.

The old must die for the new to be reborn. You began to experience the beginnings of this death/rebirth motif in your eight year. What defined your life for the previous eight years has now fallen away. You are like a cup that has been emptied of its contents, or a field that lies fallow and will not be planted till next year.

This time of resting and waiting is very hard for our ego to adjust to. We are people who define ourselves by what we do and the roles that we play. When we are stripped of these roles we feel uncomfortable, naked and exposed. That is why spiritual practice in a nine year is essential.

The first three months of the nine year are about detaching and letting go of the past. The last nine months of the nine year correspond to the zero year, which is symbolized by the in utero experience from conception to birth.

Another metaphor for the zero year is the chrysalis into which the caterpillar disappears when it is time for him to grow wings and become a butterfly. His time as a busy multilegged creature moving slowly and deliberately over the earth has come to an end. When he emerges from the chrysalis he will not be able to walk any more. He will need to learn to spread his wings and fly.

The zero year is all about the transformation of consciousness. We move from a limited state to a less limited one. As the energy inside us expands, we give birth to a form and structure that is less limiting and gives us a new freedom and ability to explore the world. It is almost like moving into a new body, which is why the metaphor of the caterpillar and the butterfly is so poignant.

The danger that faces you in the nine/zero year is that you will not allow the transformation to happen. You will hold onto the old definitions of who you are or you will live in regret for what happened. You will get stuck in the past and feel unable to forgive yourself and others. You will stay emotionally attached to the energy of the old cycle and find it difficult to let go or surrender.

However, change will come whether you want it to or not.

Either you will cooperate with your soul's need to grow and transform or you will resist the inevitable, bringing unnecessary pain and struggle into your life. A caterpillar that tries to back out of the chrysalis becomes a gluey mess. He does not have legs anymore. Trying to return to the past is impossible. The only way through the chrysalis is out the other side.

Your choice is not whether or not you want to die and be reborn. Death and rebirth are inevitable aspects of life. Your only choice is whether or not you choose to resist change or learn to surrender to it.

A nine year is a time to re-enter the silence and listen for guidance. This is not a year of action, but of non-action and reflection. It is a year in which the old self dies and the new self prepares to be born. The more you are able to let go and trust the transformational process, the easier it will be for the energy of the new cycle to manifest in your life.

WHAT NOT TO DO IN A NINE YEAR

Do not live in regret. Accept what happened. Forgive and let go.

Don't hold onto the past or resist change. It will only frustrate you and delay your eventual transformation.

Don't try to maintain your old life. It has run its course and served its purpose. Let it go.

Don't be afraid to sit with yourself. That is what is called for.

Don't judge yourself for being inactive or for needing to take a break from the affairs of the world. This is appropriate and natural in a nine year.

Don't look for something to do or somewhere to go. There is nothing to do and nowhere to go.

Don't be afraid of the silence. It is your birthing chamber.

Don't judge your emptiness. Come to God naked, empty, and without expectations.

AFFIRMATIONS FOR A NINE YEAR

⊚ I am willing to let the past go and live in the present moment.

⊚ I am committed to my spiritual practice.

⊚ I understand that the old self is dying and the new self is being born and I am patient with myself as I go through the process.

⊚ I am willing to leave the affairs of the world behind for a time and enter the inner temple.

⊚ I know that there is nothing I need to do and nowhere else I need to be.

⊚ I am not resisting change but allowing everything to unfold naturally in its own time and course.

⊚ I understand that I am moving beyond old limited patterns and gradually giving birth to a life that offers me greater freedom to be myself.

Contrasts and Continuities

THE DIFFERENCE BETWEEN A ONE YEAR AND A TWO YEAR

In a one year you are primarily nurturing yourself and your vision. You are protective of the new energy and are self-engaged and self-referenced. You aren't seeking feedback from others or comparing yourself to them. In a two year you begin comparing your ideas and vision to the ideas and vision of others, noticing and analyzing differences. This helps you to refine your vision and begin to define who you are in relationship to others. In year two you may seek feedback from others and begin to gather the information you need to make your ideas practical and relevant to others.

HOW A THREE YEAR BUILDS ON A TWO YEAR

In a two year you look at what others are doing, refine your vision and become clear on your direction. In a three year you begin actively communicating and sharing that vision with others. You build alliances and enter into relationships that can help you implement your vision in the world. While a two year helps you understand the context around you, it is not really an action year. On the other hand, a three year is clearly an action year. It is the first year in the cycle when your energy is really moving outward.

THE DIFFERENCE BETWEEN
A THREE YEAR AND A FOUR YEAR

In a three year you are actively communicating who you are and what you think and feel to others. You are actively cultivating relationships and building alliances. You are doing this with a wide reach, exploring all the connections that are available to you. In a four year you are narrowing your focus and making choices. You are building the foundation and structure of life. In that sense, you are already committed to the shape and form that your vision is taking as you implement it in the world.

A three year can be compared to dating around. A four year can be compared to a marriage or committed relationship. In a three year you are exploring different forms and choices. In a four year you have found the form that works best. You have made your choices and are committed to them.

HOW A FIVE YEAR BUILDS ON A FOUR YEAR

In a four year you have anchored the vision into physical reality. Hard work and diligence have given the vision a form. Discipline and follow through have given the form functionality. But in a four year there is always the tendency to become lost in the details and to be unable to step back and see the big picture. In a five year you step back and look at what you have created. You get perspective and see how the form can be opened up so that it is not limiting or restrictive.

A five year is a year of growth and expansion. It breathes new life and greater flexibility into the structure you have created.

THE DIFFERENCE BETWEEN A FIVE YEAR AND A SIX YEAR

In a five year, you are expanding the form so that you are not limited by it. You are taking risks, exploring new directions and possibilities that will give new life and energy to the commitments you have already made. You are giving yourself the freedom to explore, expand your consciousness and individuate.

In a six year, you are finding ways to incorporate your personal growth into your family structure and community life. To the extent that you have outgrown certain roles and relationships that used to provide support and social context for you, you are now seeking new communities that are more in alignment with the person you have grown to be.

A five year is "all about me and my unique needs." A six year is all about "how I fit in and respond to the needs of the people who share my life." A five year is about freedom and personal growth. A six year is about social responsibility and belonging.

HOW A SEVEN YEAR BUILDS ON A SIX YEAR

In a six year you create harmony and community with others who share your interests and values. You establish a support system and a network of friends and colleagues who understand and promote your work. This gives you the visibility that you need to move your work forward with energy and enthusiasm.

In a seven year you find the audience you need and begin sharing with confidence. You begin to shine your light unabashedly.

THE DIFFERENCE BETWEEN
A SEVEN YEAR AND AN EIGHT YEAR

In a seven year, you are actively expressing yourself in the world. Your cup is full to the brim. Your creativity is in full force and you are moving forward with self-confidence. This is a year when you are shining your light and other people are noticing and acknowledging you.

In an eight year, your energy shifts inward and you begin learning the lessons that arise from the active years of your cycle (years 3-7). You may have crossed boundaries and stepped on the toes of others. Not everyone has been impacted in a positive way by all your activity and you need time to learn from your mistakes and forgive your trespasses.

No matter how much success comes in your seven year, some aspects of your life may have gone out of balance and you need to take time to heal and come back into alignment. Your cup is now almost empty and attempting to give to and take care of others is counterproductive. This is a time for you to rest, recharge, reconcile and forgive.

HOW A NINE YEAR BUILDS ON AN EIGHT YEAR

In an eight year your energy and attention begin to move inward. You heal, forgive and come back into balance. That prepares you for the detachment that is called for in your nine year, when you relinquish the past, gradually withdraw from the affairs of the world and prepare to give birth to a new energy and vision of self.

THE DIFFERENCE BETWEEN
A NINE YEAR AND A ONE YEAR

In a nine year, you begin to detach from the drama of the previous cycle. You let go of the past so that you can make room for the new energy that wants to come into your life. This is not a time for doing, but a time to refrain from action. You withdraw from the affairs of the world in order to find a safe place where you can allow the old to die and the new to be born. This is especially true of the last 9 months of the nine year (the zero year).

In a one year, the old energy has moved out and the new energy has come in. It is unknown and innocent, like a baby, and you need to welcome it and nurture it. Slowly, you get in touch with who you are and begin to take baby steps back into the world. While the nine year is about detachment and withdrawal from the world, the one year is about the slow, gradual re-engagement with the outside world.

TABLE 1

The Nine Cycles of Nine Years

1	2	3	4	5	6	7	8	9
0-1	1-2	2-3	3-4	4-5	5-6	6-7	7-8	8-9
9-10	**10-11**	11-12	12-13	13-14	14-15	15-16	16-17	17-18
18-19	19-20	**20-21**	21-22	22-23	23-24	24-25	25-26	`26-27
27-28	28-29	29-30	**30-31**	31-32	32-33	33-34	34-35	`35-36
36-37	37-38	38-39	39-40	**40-41**	41-42	42-43	43-44	44-45
45-46	46-47	47-48	48-49	49-50	**50-51**	51-52	52-53	53-54
54-55	55-56	56-57	57-58	58-59	59-60	**60-61**	61-62	62-63
63-64	64-65	65-66	66-67	67-68	68-69	69-70	**70-71**	71-72
72-73	73-74	74-75	75-76	76-77	77-78	78-79	79-80	**80-81**

Numbers in bold type are numinous or quintessential years.

3

PART THREE

From Birth to Age Eighty-One

A WORD OF CAUTION

Writing a description of the meaning of all 81 years in the nine cycles of nine years is a monumental task. There is simply no way to capture all of the psychological themes that may be arising in a person's life in any given year.

So I must offer these descriptions to you with the caveat that they cannot possibly do justice to the complexity of your life or anyone else's life. Please use each description as a finger pointing toward truth and do not regard it as truth itself. If you use your understanding of each of the nine principles presented in Part 2 of this book, along with your intuition about what is happening in your life, you will be able to see the bigger picture.

Just reading the description and trying to fit your life into it will not bring accurate understanding. When reading any description in Part 3, please consider what is said and use your intuition to integrate what you have read with the actual events and circumstances unfolding in your life.

For Part 3 to be empowering to you, you must bring to these readings a solid understanding of the 9 principles discussed in Part 2, as well as your own patient inquiry. Taking the time to integrate and synthesize the psychological themes that you find on these pages with the details of your life can lead to insight and sometimes even revelation.

Do not expect this book to do all the work for you. A tool is just a tool. It is up to you to learn how to use it skillfully so that you have a better understanding of what life is asking of you at any stage of your journey.

00-09

Early Childhood Years

1ST YEAR (00-01)

Your first year begins with your birth into the physical world. You arrive innocent. Yet you may have experienced some kind of discomfort or trauma in the womb or in your birth experience. Or perhaps you were born sick or weak and had to be kept in the hospital away from your parents.

Even if your gestation and birth was uneventful, you probably experienced some kind of disorientation entering the physical world. Birth is one of the great transitions in life and coming into a body has many challenges.

Although you now inhabit a separate body from your mommy's, you are still fused with her in many ways. If mommy enjoys being a mommy, this fusion will be a positive thing for you. If you are successfully breast fed, if you are held and touched and given lots of physical affection, your bonding with mommy will continue and you will receive the nurturing you need to thrive.

On the other hand, if mommy does not like being a

mommy, if she is stressed out and overwhelmed, or if she has post-partum depression, you may not get the nurturing you need. Then you may begin to internalize the message that you are not loveable.

This first year of your life will provide many physical challenges as you learn to gain control over your basic movements and reflexes. There will also be emotional challenges as you experience separation anxiety when mommy moves away, and you learn to call her back by crying and getting her attention. Depending on how attentive mommy is, you may move easily through these challenges or you may have difficulty and your emotional health and growth can be negatively affected.

In the first year of your life, you learn to crawl and explore your environment. You begin to take your first steps toward independent existence.

2ND YEAR (00-01)

Your second year of life is when you will probably learn to stand on your own and begin to walk and explore the outside world. You will start to encounter the world on your own terms. This is an important sign of independence. Your curiosity is literally given legs.

The second year is also a time you may push back against their parents and siblings in an attempt to define who you are. Your need to say "no" to mommy or daddy or siblings is an attempt to self-validate or verify your boundaries.

Your two year begins a quest for knowledge of self. While the one year represents fusion with the parents in an attempt to meet your primary needs, the two year is about discovering the physical and emotional limits that let you know where others end and you begin. You are establishing the territory of self not just outwardly, but inwardly as well, as you begin to encounter an inner world of consciousness (thoughts, feelings, etc) that belong only to you.

Your two year can be experienced negatively if you are unable to establish boundaries between self and other and/or you are not able to begin to explore the world around you. In this case, you may stay fused, merged or dependent on your parents in a way that prevents you from developing naturally. By contrast, it is also possible in a two year that you may experience too many boundaries or limits that are too rigid or harsh. That tends to create a lack of emotional safety and you may feel isolated or cut off from love in a way that is not healthy.

3RD YEAR (02-03)

In your third year of life you find your voice. You increase your vocabulary and learn to speak sentences. This year is all about communication. Developing language enables you to interact with others. You learn to tell others what you want and need and you begin to listen to their needs and wants. Now there is an increased awareness of "self" and "other" and how your needs and desires can complement those of other people or be in conflict with them.

In your third year you are actively exploring relationships and learning the joy of sharing and connection, as well as the disappointment of fighting and disconnection. The interpersonal skills that you learn this year will greatly shape your ability to interact with others in the future.

If you are lucky, your parents are good role models of healthy communication both in their relationship with each other and with you. If you have siblings, the ability of the parents to support all of you equally, without taking sides, begins to build a consciousness of fairness and abundance (knowing there is enough time and attention for everyone). On the other hand, if your parents fight with each other and with you, if they take sides, favor one child over another, you will not have very good role models for future relationships.

This is a year when you learn to tell others who you are and actively share your experiences. It is also a time when you learn to be aware of and sensitive to the needs of others. A successful three year lays the foundation for developing superior communication skills and experiencing success in your future relationships.

4TH YEAR (03-04)

In your fourth year of life you complete your mastery of your bodily functions. You are toilet trained and have good control over your motor skills. You get around well in your home and on the playground where you can climb, slide, swing, skip, jump, and run around. You have good self esteem, know how to stand up for yourself, and are confident about accomplishing your daily activities. Your vocabulary and other language skills have increased, you learn to count objects and you are curious about how things work in the world.

During the fourth year of your life you learn to make your home in your body and in the physical world. You build the foundation for your life as an independent person. You feel safe and secure in your world. That safety and security give you the confidence to reach out into larger world where you will encounter your peers and adults other than your parents in new ways and in new environments.

To the extent that you experience illness or trauma that interrupts or undermines your ability to feel comfortable in your body and immediate home environment, you may lack confidence going forward. You may be overprotected by your parents and be timid about taking on new challenges that require you to learn new skills. Lack of safety and security in year four can have a far reaching effect on your subsequent development, making it difficult for you to succeed in school and other social environments.

5TH YEAR (04-05)

In your five year you begin to explore both the outer and inner world. You interact with other children, play actively and develop your creativity by making up stories or by creating imaginary friends. If you attend preschool, your world expands greatly and you become more independent. This is a time when you are asking a lot of questions and actively trying to understand the world around you. If your parents are supportive, they will stay close when you need them and give you the space to grow and learn on your own.

If your parents are overprotective, they will set rigid limits and deny you the freedom that you need to explore the world. You may internalize the message that "the world is not a safe place" and you may be afraid to be independent and to take risks. As a result you will not develop confidence in yourself and this can have a lasting impact on your life.

On the other hand, if your parents are under-protective, they may push you out of the nest before you are ready or be dismissive of your fears and separation anxiety. This can result in your not feeling safe in pre-school or other new environments and you may begin to act out or to shut down emotionally.

Both over-protection and under-protection can be wounding and arrest your normal development. Instead of expanding creatively, and enthusiastically embracing new experiences, you pull back into yourself and isolate from others. You do not learn to trust yourself or the world around you.

They key to a good five year is getting emotional support

from your parents while they also encourage you to step out into the world. That combination of caring, protection, and encouragement from parents and other adults enables you to build confidence in yourself and contributes greatly to your success in life.

6TH YEAR (05-06)

By the time you are five and begin your sixth year you have usually started kindergarten and are exploring a whole new social environment. This may be the first time you experience a social unit apart from home and it can be a challenging time, as you try to learn how to fit in with your peers. You work hard to understand and play by the rules and may be judgmental about other children who have difficulty accepting norms. Of course, sometimes you say or do something that is not accepted by your peers and teachers, and you may feel shame or embarrassment.

If your parents are supportive, they help you adjust to the new social environment and process all of the new ideas and behaviors you are learning. They encourage you to accept and learn from your mistakes and to give other children the benefit of the doubt. They make it clear to you that accepting differences and getting along with other children is important and that bullying or shaming others is not acceptable.

During your sixth year you learn about social norms and try to conform to them and live up to what is expected of you. Your capacity to accept these norms and fit in with others, or your need to struggle against norms and stand out as an individual will have a major impact on your future social development. Some children so much want to be liked by other children that they easily develop a mask and form cliques that exclude other girls or boys who are less popular. Other children may be shy and feel awkward interacting with others and they may be ostracized, shamed or bullied.

Ideally your parents help you to find a balance between being yourself and being with others. They encourage you to talk about your successes and failures in kindergarten and to discuss how some of the norms and expectations are different there than they are at home.

If you are naturally gregarious, you will tend to shine at school and will need to learn to be sensitive to the needs and feelings of others. If you are very sensitive and tend to be a loner, you will need to learn to speak up and stand up for yourself and reach out to other children. Either way, there is much to learn in your sixth year.

7TH YEAR (06-07)

In your seventh year of life you are off to elementary school. If you have already been to pre-school and kindergarten, then this transition may not be too difficult, as you will already have confidence in your ability to interact with your peers and your teachers. If this is the first year you have been out of the home, it may be a challenging year for you, as you learn to adjust to a whole new social environment. Without previous social and intellectual stimulation, you may lag behind your peers and lack confidence in yourself.

This is the year when you will learn to read and to write or, if you already know how to do this, you will begin to show your mastery of these important communication skills. If your parents have read to you and spent time helping you learn to read you will master these skills quickly and be a confident learner. That confidence will help you shine amongst your peers and you will receive recognition from your peers and your teachers.

On the other hand, lack of educational and social support from parents can handicap you, cause you to feel inferior to your peers and lead to behavioral difficulties like bullying other children to compensate for your inferiority.

Developing self esteem is one of the most important aspects of this year. This is a year when you begin to understand and express your talents and gifts or you hold back because you are afraid of criticism. If you have critical parents who push you and tell you that what you say or do is not good enough, you will have a hard time at school. You may internalize your parents' perfectionism and even when you do well you may still feel that it is not good enough.

The degree to which you gain confidence in yourself and develop healthy self-esteem will have a profound effect on your subsequent experience at school and in life in general.

8TH YEAR (07–08)

In your eighth year you begin to grapple with, digest and internalize your experience. Your focus shifts from the outside to the inside. Now your experience is not just about what you did to others or what others did to you, but about "how you think and feel about it." How you hold your experience—the way you perceive it and frame it and how you feel about it (feeling upset, triggered, guilty, judging it as good or bad, fair or unfair)—is as important as what actually happened. This overlay of thoughts and feelings on experience (the world of perception) creates a more complex world.

Your eighth year is a time when you will begin to develop psychological depth and complexity. You will sometimes withdraw from parents and peers so that you can come to terms with something that happened that upset you or pushed your buttons. You may feel guilty about something that you said or did. You may learn to forgive yourself or one of your friends or teachers. You may get sick or have an accident and have to learn to rest and to heal.

Ideally, in your eighth year, you become aware of the consequences of your actions and begin to understand on some level that you are responsible for the choices that you make. On the other hand, you may have trouble acknowledging your mistakes and may avoid or deny responsibility for your thoughts and actions, preferring to blame others. Rather than beginning to acknowledge your shadow, you begin to project it outward, judging and finding fault with others, instead of looking at your own pain and discomfort.

This is the year when you may develop some of the defense mechanisms and other forms of denial that create interpersonal strife and internal conflict that can deepen throughout your life. If your parents, teachers, therapists or other significant adult role models can create a safe space for you to come to terms with your thoughts and feelings and express your pain, your guilt and your confusion, you will begin to find ways to acknowledge and learn from your mistakes, forgive yourself and others, and come to peace within yourself. In this sense, this may be the most important year of learning in your life. It establishes—or fails to establish—a pathway for going within and learning to understand and accept your experience. In your eighth year you learn to adjust, heal and come back into balance, or you don't. You discover that pain is a wake up call and you heed the call, or you ignore it and try to hide your pain. That sets the tone for the rest of your life.

9TH YEAR (08-09)

This is the last year of your first cycle. Like all nine years, this is a year of completion and detachment. Your early childhood is over and you are getting ready to make your transition to adolescence. Soon big changes will be happening in your body, as you go through puberty.

In your ninth year you may withdraw a bit from friends and family. While your parents may be concerned that you are isolating, spending time by yourself and connecting with your inner experience is extremely helpful at this time. You have spent the last eight years learning about the world and mastering control of your physical body. Now it is time to take a bit of a rest from constant outward activity to tune into who you are and what you need. This is especially true of the last nine months before your ninth birthday. Like the caterpillar entering the cocoon, you are getting ready to be born into a new dimension of life.

Hopefully the adults around you can appreciate your need for introspection and self communion. Putting pressure on you to be productive, socially active and externally engaged is inappropriate now. You need time and space to go within. You may benefit from interaction with a therapist or mentor with whom you can talk about your experience.

Within every cycle there are active and productive years and years when the energy is more internal. The movement inside began in your eighth year and continues in your ninth year and well into the first year of your new cycle. Think of this as a time for recharging and re-direction. Next year will be a year of new beginnings. New challenges will present themselves. In this year of rest, quiet and gestation, you are getting emotionally prepared to show up for the next phase of your life

(09-18)

The Adolescent Years

10th YEAR (09-10)

In your tenth year, as in all one years, you will be developing a new sense of who you are. You will be drawn to new experiences and will explore new activities and friendships. You may also begin to compare yourself to others and assert your uniqueness. If you are a boy, you may feel competitive with other boys and become curious about girls. If you are a girl you may become competitive with other girls and become curious about boys. Or you may experience some ambivalence in your sexual identity.

In addition to gender differences, you may also notice differences in race, ethnic origin, religion, economic status and other factors. While it is inevitable that you will tend to define yourself based on these factors, it is also important that you learn that others, though different from you, are equal to you and just as worthy of love and acceptance as you are. Each person deserves to be who he or she is and should not be compared either favorably or unfavorably to others.

You may also notice how you are different from others in terms of your strengths and weaknesses. Some people may be physically stronger or mentally quicker than you are, while you may have greater intuitive ability and artistic talents. Again, the important thing is to accept the differences without feeling less than or better than others.

When you accept differences, you give yourself and others the freedom to be unique, multi-faceted human beings. While everyone wants to fit in and be accepted by others, there are times when you have to be true to yourself and in so doing you are going to stand out and be seen for who you are. That may mean that other people judge you or criticize you, but please understand that they do this because they are insecure about who they are.

Hopefully, you can understand and accept your uniqueness without feeling "less than" or better than" others. If so, you will establish the basis for equality in your relationships with others. And that will create a strong foundation for living a compassionate and productive life.

11 TH YEAR (10-11)

Your eleventh year is the numinous and quintessential two year. We all know and understand things in different ways. Some of us are analytical. Others are more intuitive. Some are good at seeing the big picture, but are not good at seeing details. Some see details very sharply but cannot see the big picture. Some people know in words, others in sounds or pictures. For some, the mind is dominant and the intellect shines. For others, the heart is dominant and feelings are key.

As you move into your second two year, it becomes important for you to understand and honor how you know. Unfortunately, you may not get much support or encouragement from parents and teachers. They have their own idea of who you are or who you should strive to be. These ideas have more to do with their own story than they do with yours. Yet it can be hard to find the truth about you when others expect you to fulfill their own aspirations and agendas.

You are successful in this important year if you can learn to see and value your own learning style. That means refusing to be limited or handicapped by external standards imposed by teachers and other authority figures. Your way of learning is unique and must be accepted. Labels like ADHD, Dyslexic, Autistic, etc. are helpful only if they assist you in better understanding both your challenges and your strengths. You may have paranormal abilities that other people experience as strange or threatening. In one way or another, you know that you are different and you are challenged in this year to accept and work with the unique abilities that you have.

With any luck, your parents and teachers are supportive of you and encourage you to learn in the way that works best for you. Perhaps it becomes clear in this year that you need to be in a school that allows for different learning styles.

The key to the eleventh year of your life is celebrating the unique way that you process and gather information. Your way might be quite different than the way of your peers. If you judge yourself for being different, it may be difficult for you to move forward developmentally. This year is a time to learn to accept your learning style and see the gifts that it can bring to yourself and others.

12TH YEAR (11-12)

Your twelfth year focuses on learning to communicate and interact with your peers, siblings, parents and teachers. It is important for you to learn to express your thoughts and feelings in an honest, non-blaming way. People need to be able to see you and hear you clearly. Don't be afraid to speak up, but realize that other people have their own experience and they hear things based on their own filters and interpretations. Their ability to hear you also depends on whether or not you have triggered some fear in them. When someone is triggered they see only themselves in you. They don't see you. Understand that some of your peers may have judgments about you that are not accurate. Try not to take this personally and react to their judgments. You know who you are. Keep letting others know what is true for you and what is not.

You also have judgments about your peers. Sometimes they trigger you and you cannot really see them or hear them. Try to be aware of that when you find yourself reacting to something your friends say or do. Realize that when you react in anger or hurt toward someone, it is usually because you see part of yourself in them and it is usually something about yourself that you don't like. So you are really judging yourself, not them. In fact, you don't really see them.

That is why it is important for you to learn about the shadow. This is the part of you that you don't like or accept. Everybody has a shadow. Everybody has some part of themselves that they don't like or accept.

Your challenge is to learn to accept everything that is true about you, including the shadow parts of you that you don't like. If you can accept these parts of you, you won't project them onto others or react when they project their shadow parts onto you. Of course, this is not easy to do. It takes a lot of practice to learn how to take responsibility for your own perceptions, instead of blaming others.

Clear non-blaming communication is an art that must be learned. We do not always say what we mean or mean what we say. We see other people through the lens of our own judgments. And behind every judgment is some fear or insecurity that we have. That does not make us wrong or bad. It just means that we haven't learned to love all of ourselves yet.

Judging, calling names, saying bad things about other people only leads to pain and separation. It is important to stop doing that. When others attack you or say something that is hurtful to you, it means that they are hurting inside. Try to see that and feel compassion for them. Remind yourself that there are times when you are hurting and you strike out against others.

All of us have hurts inside and sometimes they are triggered by other people. All of us strike out and trespass against others. When you feel hurt or anger, try to be aware of it and realize there is fear coming up. Ask yourself "what am I afraid of? Why am I feeling shamed or rejected?" These kinds of questions will help you realize what needs to be healed inside yourself. Then you won't react automatically and attack others.

By taking responsibility for your own hurt and pain, you will get along much better with others. They will feel that you are a good and caring friend and enjoy spending time with you. When they are triggered and take their anger out on you, you will learn not to take it personally. You will know that it is "their stuff," not yours. Then you can feel compassion for them and offer them forgiveness, love and acceptance. This is how you learn to be a peacemaker.

13TH YEAR (12-13)

In your thirteenth year of your life you are starting to enter puberty and to experience some of the sexual awakenings associated with it (although in some young people this occurs earlier and in some later). It is important that the changes that are happening in your body and in your emotions are compassionately acknowledged by your parents, your teachers, your doctor and other significant adults in your life, so that you do not feel anxiety or shame around them. You need to feel comfortable asking questions about ovulation, pregnancy, birth control, and other subjects associated with this change of life so that you have the information and perspective that you need and do not feel overwhelmed by the changes that are occurring.

If your sexual awakening is not dealt with openly by parents and other significant adults, your experience of this important change of life may be difficult and fraught with guilt, shame and emotional instability. This is even more true if you experience any kind of sexual abuse or inappropriate behavior from adults or peers.

By now you are probably fairly confident interacting with your peers and feeling safe and secure in your school environment. Your learning style and communication patterns have become clear, you know what is expected of you at school, and you have stabilized mentally and emotionally. You have built a solid foundation that you will gradually build on as you move on to higher learning and skill development.

Your thirteen year should be a stable year for you at school and at home. As such it should provide you with a reliable structure and routine that enables you to handle some of the internal changes that are happening for you. If this is not the case, it is important to get outside assistance from teachers, doctors and/or therapists who can help you adjust to hormonal changes that may be distracting you.

14TH YEAR (13-14)

If you did not already move into secondary school last year, you will be doing so in your fourteenth year. Hopefully by now you have developed your self confidence and have learned to take risks in your life. If so, you will welcome the opportunity to have a wider range of experiences. Having built the foundation by learning basic skills in language, mathematics and other core subjects, you will now have the opportunity to explore those areas where you have special talents and gifts.

Your fourteenth year should be a year of intellectual and creative expansion. You will learn many new subjects, take new creative risks, and begin to individuate as a person. You will understand and move naturally toward what you are most interested in and good at.

It is important that you do this in a playful and joyful way. Putting too much pressure on yourself to achieve will interfere with the creative process and cause you to tighten up. So try to take the pressure off and take small steps forward until you feel confident in yourself.

Your fourteenth year is also a time when you may become interested in the arts and or in spirituality. You may join a choir or theater group or become active in a youth group at your church or synagogue or mosque. Anything that takes you out into the world and offers you new experiences is important.

This year and the one previous correspond to the onset of puberty and to the rites of passage that happen as you make the transition from childhood to adulthood. The fact that you become of age sexually, that you go from being a child to being capable of making a child, marks an important milestone in your life. It also underscores your potential for creativity, for bringing something new into the world.

In your fourteenth year, it is important for you "to know yourself" in a deeper way, to discover and begin to express your unique talents and gifts, to learn to trust your capacity to create the kind of life that you desire and aspire to. You become aware of what you value the most. You begin to explore the concept of God and to look for meaning and purpose in your life.

15TH YEAR (14–15)

In your fifteenth year you experience the power of peer pressure and it becomes important for you be popular and fit in. You try hard to observe social norms about what clothing or music is popular. You are also beginning to compete with other girls or boys for the attention of the opposite sex.

In your fifteenth year, you find out whether you are a conformist or a non-conformist, whether you accept social rules and norms or whether you feel that you must reject them and uphold your individuality. While you want to be accepted by your peers, you may be painfully aware of how you are different and don't fit in. This brings your first real identify challenge. Do you develop a mask and pretend to be like others so that they will accept you, or do you realize that you have to be true to yourself?

Few young people are able to stand up to peer pressure and give themselves permission to be different. The extent to which you stand up for yourself will determine the degree to which you individuate in this new nine year cycle.

On the other hand, it is important for you not to isolate yourself and allow others to define you. Have the courage to reach out and let other people know who you are. Join the acting club, the chorus, the debating team or the basketball team. Become a scout, a volunteer or a member of the youth group at your church or synagogue. Be part of something larger than yourself. Your growth in the cycle is also measured by the degree to which you come out of your shell and interact with others.

Try to find a balance between being yourself and being with others. Hopefully, your parents, teachers or other role models in your life will help you find your social bearings during this year. They will encourage you to open up and talk about your experiences so that you can move through any fear or shame that is coming up for you.

In your fifteenth year you continue to come to terms with your sexuality and begin to accept (or struggle with) the fact that you are attracted to girls or to boys. Your comfort or discomfort with your sexuality and the degree to which you feel able to socialize easily with others in the gender of choice can define much of what this year will be about for you.

16TH YEAR (15-16)

Sweet sixteen happens for those who have built their confidence and self-esteem through their early childhood years. This is the year when it is time for you to shine by expressing your talents and gifts. If you feel supported by family and friends and you have experienced previous success in school, you will have a solid foundation on which you can build this year.

If you are confident in your abilities, you will not be afraid let other people see who you are and what you can do. Even if you are shy you will find a way to move through your resistance and allow yourself to be seen and heard. On the other hand, if you have internalized perfectionist tendencies from your parents and you feel you can never do it right, you will not be at ease in your self expression and it will not flow for you. Your doubts and fears will seem huge and you will be afraid of making a mistake and being rejected by others.

This is a year when you need to understand that mistakes are part of the learning process and it is only by risking failure that you can succeed in life.

So try to take the pressure off yourself. Just do the best you can and know that it will be good enough. Even if you make a mistake it will be okay. It will just make you stronger.

Your biggest challenge in your sixteenth year is to learn to believe in yourself and to trust your talents and gifts. If you are scared or lack confidence, start by taking baby steps toward your goal. Surround yourself with people who are supportive of you. As you succeed with small steps, you will be ready to take on bigger challenges.

17TH YEAR (16–17)

Your seventeenth year is a time when introspection is called for, yet you may experience a lot of pressure to stay engaged in school and social activities. Don't be concerned if you begin to withdraw from the expectations of others. This may be a year when you become clear on how you don't fit in with or feel emotionally connected to your peers. They may make judgments about you or you about them. You may feel that others do not accept and appreciate you as you are. You may even be ostracized by your peers.

Coming to terms with and accepting the differences between yourself and others, affirming your own experience, and cultivating a connection with your inner guidance is essential this year. In order to do this, you need to turn within so that you can forgive yourself or others, heal wounds or hurt feelings, recover from an accident or illness and learn to be gentle with yourself.

Give yourself the time that you need to rest and recharge. Get counseling or support if you need it. This year is the beginning of the transition to a new nine year phase of your life. It begins with healing and rebalancing this year and continues with detachment and completion next year so that eventually the slate can be wiped clean and you can start again.

During the next two years your adolescence will come to an end and you will be ready to enter your young adult years. This is the time when you begin to end your dependency on your parents and need to have the freedom to find out who you are as a separate person. There is always some tension and growing pain in the process, as you make your gradual transition out of childhood into adulthood.

18TH YEAR (17–18)

Don't be surprised if you need to set some limits with your parents and your friends in your eighteenth year. This is the last year of your adolescence and you are getting ready to move into adulthood. It may also be your last year of secondary school. You have decisions to make about whether to go to college, find a job, and find your own place to live, etc.

Adults may expect you to have the answer already about what your next step is. But don't be surprised if you don't really know which direction to take. This year is about wrapping things up, detaching and completing. It is not a year that involves moving forward. In fact, you may need to take an extended time to get quiet and reflect on where you have been and where you feel inclined to go.

Taking time in meditation, walking in nature, or just spending time by yourself helps you get in touch with your feelings and begin to find a direction from the inside out.

The transition to adulthood is a profound one. Young people are not given the "sacred time and space" or "rite of passage" that they need to move through this death/rebirth experience. Far too much pressure is put on them and, as a result, they often make commitments before they are ready. Their choices are unduly influenced by the expectations of parents, teachers or even peers, and are not necessarily in harmony with their own unique needs, desires and talents. That is tragic and unnecessary.

Don't let that happen to you. This year is a time when you can finish your school work and come to peace with the choices that you have made so far in your life. "Detaching" is just as important as "completing." This is not a year to take on new commitments, because you simply do not know yet what you need.

Don't allow yourself to be pressured by the adults around you. Ask for the time and space you need. Ask your parents to back off and respect your boundaries. Ask for their support and understanding this year. Ask them to be patient with you as you figure things out. And be patient with yourself.

It doesn't work to push the river. Wait until you feel ready to jump in and then the river will carry you.

(18-27)

The Young Adult Years

19TH YEAR (18-19)

Your nineteenth year is a time when you may leave home and go away to school, move into your own apartment and begin a new job, or embark on a journey to explore the world. It is a year of risk taking and growth. You are beginning to live your own life apart from your family. You are learning to be with others on your own terms.

Communicating who you are honestly to others is very important. It establishes the basis for healthy relationships. It is quite possible that an important relationship will come into your life this year. The success of that relationship will depend on your feeling that you can be yourself with that person and learn to honor the other person's needs as well as your own. The big question for both people in any relationship is "Can I be myself and be with you?"

If the answer is "yes' the relationship will thrive and be a vehicle for both of you to discover who you are. If the answer is "no," you will move on to other relationships in which you endeavor to be authentic and true to yourself. You will learn a lot about what communication skills you have (or lack and need to learn) and what some of your greatest challenges are when you are in a relationship.

In your nineteenth year, you are exploring who you are in relationship to others. You are defining yourself in a new way, as a person who is no longer dependent on or seeking to please your parents. This is a year when you will learn a lot about yourself and begin to develop a new vision of where you want to go in the coming eight years.

20 TH YEAR (19–20)

In your twentieth year, you begin to get clear on your direction for the remainder of the cycle and you begin to study, plan and prepare for the future. That might be college or work, or yet another adventure.

If you began an important relationship last year, the relationship may be tested this year, as your partner begins to trigger old wounds from your childhood.

The first tendency that you have when triggered is to make it be the other person's fault. That is an attempt to project your own fear and shame on your partner. Your partner does the same when you trigger him or her.

So now there are not just two adults having a relationship. There are two wounded children who are fighting, blaming and shaming each other. Your reactive patterns—fight, flight or shut down emotionally—and those of your partner seem to be running the show. Needless to say the days of romance are quickly over.

While you may hope that another's love will bring greater happiness into your life, the reality is that no one is able to love you more than you love yourself. So all of the ways in which you are blocked and afraid of love and intimacy are bound to surface in your relationship. When romance ends the harsh reality of fear and shame—the domain of the shadow—rise up and with them all of the defense mechanisms you have built up to try to keep you safe.

Ironically perhaps, the very behaviors which are designed to protect you actually prevent you from experiencing intimacy. This is a year in which you need to learn to see the shadow side of yourself and your partner with understanding and compassion. Going to a good therapist—especially if your relationship is in crisis—can help. Studying psychology, reading self-help books, going to couples workshops are all constructive activities that can bring greater awareness of the unconscious wounds that you need to heal in order to create a harmonious relationship.

21 ST YEAR (20-21)

This is your quintessential three year. It is a time when you are actively communicating with others who share your interests and values. It is a time to come out of your shell, if you have one, and join the dance.

If you are not already in a relationship, this is often a year when you can meet someone who could become a long term partner. Try to take the time to get to know potential partners before you make a commitment. It is important that you and the other person have shared experiences and values and learn how to communicate well. Be patient, spend quality time together, and talk in depth so that you choose your partner wisely.

Moreover, learn to accept the differences between you. Realize that no one person is going to meet all of your needs or agree with you all of the time. Each person has a different mindset and different life experiences. Don't throw away a good relationship because you have unrealistic expectations of the other person. Learn to accept and respect where the other person is coming from and your relationship can thrive.

Inevitably conflicts arise in every relationship. People who are close trigger each other's wounds and beliefs. When triggered, your behavior and that of your partner become reactive. You may attack each other, push each other away, leave, or shut down emotionally. This doesn't mean that your relationship does not work. It simply means that the real work of the relationship is now presenting itself. Are you and your partner mature and committed enough to do the psychological work that will be required to move through your triggers to a deeper and more profound love?

Often young people abandon perfectly good relationships because they are immature and have unrealistic expectations of each other. If you love your partner, try to hang in there together and learn to take responsibility for your own wounds and triggers. Don't try to make your partner responsible for the hurts inside of you. But learn to share those hurts so that your partner can know you more deeply.

The Affinity Process (see my book *Living in the Heart*) offers you a powerful tool for taking responsibility for your thoughts, feelings, words and actions. That way you do not blame and shame your partner when fear or shame arise within you.

An intimate relationship provides both people with one of the most intense vehicles for psychological and spiritual growth available on the planet. Your partner helps you to see, embrace and begin to integrate your shadow and you do the same for her or him. If you are courageous and willing to take this journey of healing together, you will be building the foundation for a lifetime of happiness and fulfillment.

22 ND YEAR (21-22)

In your twenty-second year, you are completing college, career training, or early work experience and are getting ready to take the next step on your journey to adulthood. This is a year when you need to be very focused on what you are doing so that you can have a successful outcome.

This may also be a year in which you make a commitment to an important relationship in your life. You may decide to live together, marry or even have a child. If you have taken the time to know your partner and communicate well, you will have a reasonable chance of weathering the pressures and responsibilities that come with a committed relationship. Otherwise, the stress and emotional demands of the relationship may take your energy and focus way from activities and commitments you need to complete at work or school. In this respect, it may make more sense to live separately, even though you have both committed to the relationship. Yet only you can decide what is best for you. Having an open discussion about these issues with your partner can help you both make a choice that does not put too much pressure on you or on the relationship.

Energy needs to be focused in a four year. Discipline and routines are important. They help you to get into a productive rhythm so that you can accomplish your goals in the least stressful way. Lack of success—due to putting excessive pressure on yourself or biting off more than you can chew—can seriously undermine your confidence. In this respect, it is far better to keep your commitments modest and fulfill them with energy and purpose than to over-commit and under-perform. Taking small concrete steps toward your goal will likely to be far more effective than trying to leap frog toward your goal. Those who refuse to take baby steps and set the bar too high often crash and burn.

Every failure you experience drains you and undermines your confidence. Every success you have increases your energy and confidence. Small successes lead to larger ones. So be patient. Set reasonable goals, and put one foot in front of the other until you arrive at your destination. That is the pathway to success.

Your twenty second year is an opportunity to create the safety and security that you need in your work/career and in your relationships. Communicating with others honestly is paramount in importance. Don't be afraid to express your doubts and fears. Let people know how you feel. Bravado and over-confidence will not serve you. Getting everything out on the table helps you to see it with perspective. Take the time to tune into how you feel before you speak or act. When things happen too quickly, slow them down. That will help you avoid impulsive or reactive behavior that will make your life far more stressful and complicated than it needs to be.

23RD YEAR (22–23)

Your twenty-third year is an important time of expansion for you. If you are in a relationship, it is important that your partner understands that you need to step outside of the box and begin to explore new experiences. Giving each other the space to grow will enable the relationship to prosper. You will be able to deepen in your understanding of who you are and what you need and will bring that deeper understanding back to the relationship, breathing new energy and life into it. Without this time to explore independently, the relationship might begin to feel restrictive and you might be tempted to leave it.

If you are in a relationship with a controlling partner, you probably won't stay around very long. You will find a way to get some space, perhaps traveling abroad or going back to school somewhere distant. You may even break up or put the relationship on hold. This is often necessary if you are going to have the freedom that you need to expand your consciousness and your life experience.

While understandably you are drawn to people who share

your values and interests, this is also a year when you may venture into new relationships and meet people with different socio-economic or educational backgrounds or even people from different cultures, religions or races. This all contributes to your growth and expansion of consciousness. These new relationships may not be stable or long term, but they will be stimulating and awakening. They will help you to better understand who you are and what possible directions may be open to you in the future.

You will also be drawn to groups and activities that help you begin to develop a spiritual perspective on your life. As in all five years, you will need to move beyond limited structures at home, school or work and explore uncharted waters.

24TH YEAR (23-24)

Your twenty-fourth year is a time when you are drawn to develop a supportive community around you. Having come out of a year of expansion when you met many new people and had new experiences, you are beginning to understand who you feel comfortable with. This may include people who are different from you but share the same values and interests. This is a year when you will have an active social life, joining groups/organizations that engage in activities that you enjoy.

If you are career oriented, many of your friendships may be made at work. If you are religious, your primary social environment might be at your church or synagogue or mosque.

If you are sports oriented, you might meet people at the gym, the pool or the bicycle path.

As your life stabilizes this year, you may begin to think about whether you want to get married and have children or you may become clear that you want to continue to make school or work your primary focus. It is important that you find your own way here and not be swayed by what you think your parents, your friends, your church or society in general expects of you. If you accept and thrive on traditional values, you will cultivate a traditional lifestyle. If you are more of a non-conformist, you will be drawn to a lifestyle that expresses your creativity and uniqueness.

Whatever is right for you must be accepted, whether or not it meets the approval of others. On the other hand, what is right for you may not be right for others. You must be careful not to make judgments about others who have different values or make different lifestyle choices. Only an insecure person needs other people to have the same beliefs or make the same choices.

25TH YEAR (24–25)

Your twenty-fifth year is a year in which you can move confidently in your relationships with others. You rely on your communication skills to share your ideas and express yourself creatively. This is a great year to collaborate with others on creative projects that enable you to express your talents and gifts. It may also be a great year to commit to a relationship with someone who is empowered and can be an equal partner.

By now you are in touch with your strengths and you can see how your talents and gifts can be combined with those of others to create a synergistic experience. Acting in a play, participating in a band or orchestra, joining a dance troupe, starting a business, etc. can provide the vehicle you need to gain self confidence and learn to shine your light in the world.

On the other hand, it is not necessary for you to wait for others. Move forward when you are ready and you will attract the support and resources that you need. When you are confident in your skills and you have learned to believe in yourself, the universal energy aligns with you. Opportunities emerge without struggle. The doors open and you walk through them.

This is not a time to try to show up the way others want you to. This is a year when you need to trust who you are. Your authenticity and uniqueness attract the support of others. So give yourself permission to be yourself, do what you love to do and communicate your joy and enthusiasm to others.

26TH YEAR (25–26)

This is a year when you may be tested. Co-dependent relationships often fall apart in this year. You simply cannot expect someone else to be just like you or to meet all of your needs. Differences need to be accepted and respected. Some needs you will have to meet on your own.

Challenges can also be experienced in the areas of work. You may be disappointed when one of your creative projects fails or you are have a falling out with your boss or one of your co-workers. In addition, it is possible that an illness or health issue arises that cannot be ignored.

If you took time to move out of the box and expand your consciousness in your twenty-third year, then the lessons of this year can be minimized. Perhaps you already left a co-dependent relationship or you took a sabbatical from work. Perhaps you cut back your work schedule from 60 to 30 hours per week and began to take better care of yourself. The result would be a renewal of energy in all areas of your life, softening the impact of this eight year.

However, if you did not move out of the box in your twenty-third year, if you stayed in a controlling, co-dependent relationship, continued your workaholic behavior and intensified the stress in your life, this may be the year when your chickens come to roost. The relationship falls apart, you get fired or quit your job, and/or a health crisis or addiction arises.

Any of these events can be a wake up call for you. There are adjustments that need to be made in the way that you are living your life in order to bring it back into balance. Don't be afraid to get help from a therapist or doctor if you need assistance. If it's appropriate, join a twelve step program.

If you are struggling to communicate with your partner or if your relationships are otherwise in crisis, a counselor can help you better understand where healthy boundaries are needed in the relationship and can assist you and your partner in communicating honestly and finding common ground. Without your mutual desire to understand and improve your relationship it is likely to fall apart and create emotional pain in your life and that of your partner. In your twenty-sixth year, your relationship is either transformed from a co-dependent one to an empowered one or it comes to an end.

27TH YEAR (26-27)

This is the last year of your Young Adulthood cycle. In the last eight years you have figured out a direction in life, finished school or career training, learned to support yourself and perhaps even started a family. You have demonstrated the fact that you can live independently and no longer need to rely on your parents. Hopefully, you know now with confidence that you are the captain of your own fate. You make your own choices and reap both the rewards and the lessons.

Last year you began to look at your successes and failures and to learn the lessons that arise in your relationships with others. Often the healing/adjustment period of the eight year leads to greater detachment and time spent alone in the nine year. This is natural. Completion of the cycle often requires significant introspection as you reconcile and let go of past experience and get ready to enter a new phase of your life.

The most important lessons of this third phase that you are completing now are the lessons of relationship. Developing intimacy with another person requires strong communication skills, as well as a willingness to take responsibility for your own thoughts, words and actions. It also requires the ability to set healthy boundaries with your partner so that you both have the space you need to grow and individuate.

Rarely do we learn these skills sufficiently in the third phase of life to be successful at creating an equal, empowered relationship with another human being. Most of us make a lot of mistakes. We trigger each other and don't set healthy boundaries or we trespass on those we have set.

Of course, you may be the exception to the rule and you and your partner may survive these early years in the emotional trenches of partnership. If you are one of the few lucky couples that survive, this year will be a year in which you and your partner move into a more conscious union in which you each give the other person space to grow and individuate. As a result, the relationship can grow to a new level of trust and intimacy in the next nine year cycle.

However, don't be surprised if a significant relationship in your life went into crisis or ended last year. If so, your twenty-seventh year will be devoted to learning the lessons of that relationship and detaching emotionally so that you can regain your balance and be ready to enter the new cycle.

If you have not become economically and emotionally independent of your parents, last year may have brought a crisis in your relationship with them and you may now realize that you need to relinquish financial support in order to loosen their control over you and gain the freedom to make your own decisions. If you have not already done so, detaching from your parents so that you can begin to create your own life may become one of the primary themes of your twenty-seventh year. By cutting the umbilical cord that ties you to your parents, you usher in a new nine year cycle of self-determination and empowerment.

(27-36)

Stable Adult Years

28TH YEAR (27-28)

This is a year when you are engaged in building the foundation of your life as a self-supporting adult. Your apprenticeship years are over and it is time for you to move out into the world and create the kind of life that you want.

Like all one years, this is a year when you are beginning to tune into your direction for the next nine years. You do not necessarily know what you want to do and it is important not to put a lot of pressure on yourself to decide before you are ready.

This is a year to have new adventures and to explore a variety of activities. In your twenty eighth year, you are ordering the appetizers, not the main course of your meal of life. That comes later. It will take as long as three years for the main course to be ordered up and served. So be patient. Taste the possibilities, explore the opportunities that present themselves, walk through the open doors and see where they lead.

Give yourself time to see what feels right. Try things on for size before you commit to them. Ask yourself "Is this in harmony with who I am?" and if the answer is "no" or "maybe" do not despair. You don't have to pin everything down right now. You just need to work on getting clear on your vision of what you want the next nine years to be.

In your outer life, enjoy connecting with new friends and exploring new interests. Enjoy the moment, but also be aware that the connections you make may be stepping stones that help you crystallize your vision and move toward your long-term goals.

In your inner life, allow yourself to brainstorm, to fantasize and to dream. Allow the picture of what you want to take shape. This is not a time to try to figure out all the details. It is a time to paint with broad strokes. Next year you will have time to refine your vision. Don't put pressure on yourself to do that now.

In your twenty-eighth year you are opening up your heart and your mind to what will be one of the most powerful times of your life. During your fourth cycle of nine years, which begins this year, you will probably make some of the major decisions of your life such as what career to choose, whom to marry or live with, whether or not to have children, where to live and what kind of lifestyle you aspire to.

It is important that you make these decisions without pressure from parents, teachers or peers. Their expectations and dreams for you may not be appropriate for you. You are not here to live out their dreams but to discover and live out your own. In the process of discovery, you may have times when you are foggy or uncertain. Often that is the case because you are listening to others instead of listening to your core self. When you let yourself sink into the truth within and affirm your unique talents and gifts, then the dream begins to take shape and the course of action becomes clear.

29TH YEAR (28-29)

Whereas last year was a year for exploring new opportunities and developing a vision for your life, this year is a time when you will begin to work out some of the practical details that will be necessary to bring that vision into physical reality. You will be doing research and gathering needed knowledge so that you are prepared to communicate that vision to others (next year) and move toward its implementation (in the following year). All of this is an organic process.

Last year was a year for dreaming and brainstorming. This is a year for gathering information and analyzing it. In many respects you are playing devil's advocate and looking at potential objections or obstacles to making your vision real. You are asking questions, consulting with experts who are more experienced than you. In other words, you are doing your homework so that you will be prepared to take the test that will come next year.

You do not want to go out into the world unprepared or you run the risk of being dismissed as naïve. When you talk with others, you need to know what you are talking about. So the time spent in study and preparation this year is essential for the success of your project.

While it is necessary to analyze and compare, it is also

important to stay in touch with your intuition. Otherwise, you may begin to lose touch with the creative energy behind the vision. Both a clear mind and an open heart are necessary as you begin to pin things down. You want the form to fit the content. You don't want to force the content into a form that prevents it from expressing naturally.

30TH YEAR (29–30)

Your thirtieth year is the year when you experience your Saturn return, which symbolizes the transition from early adulthood to your stable adult years. In other words, this is the year when you start to get serious about being a self-supporting adult. You have had two years to get clear on what you want to do and to gather the needed information so that you are prepared to move forward. Now you are ready to begin communicating your vision to others.

By now you are ready to begin to take on some of the major responsibilities of life. You move forward actively with your career and very likely commit to a relationship. You may even get married and consider starting a family.

Your communication skills are very important both at work and at home. Good communication with others helps you to build the alliances you need at work and enables you to keep your relationship healthy.

Emotional stability is essential in your thirtieth year of life. You need to be sure that you are not making commitments to a relationship, work or family out of sacrifice or duty. Commitments should be made because you want to make them and they provide a necessary structure for your life.

Being in a relationship with someone you don't love, doing work that you hate, or starting a family just because others expect you to "act responsibly" will backfire in the end. If your heart is not in it, it won't work, so don't go down that road. Don't make commitments that you cannot keep or create a structure that you can't live happily with. If you do, you will be creating a prison that you will have to escape from.

On the other hand, understand that everyone has fears of intimacy and commitment. Don't expect it to be perfect. It never is. Whenever you really want something, you have to be willing to work for it and with it. Commitments are made over time as we keep showing up for the people and things that are important to us. That doesn't mean that we don't have doubts or don't get discouraged when obstacles arise. Of course, we do. But we learn to dance around obstacles and push through our resistance so that we can keep everything moving.

There are no perfect relationships or careers. Relationships and careers have good days and bad days. To prosper, they require patience, persistence, and resilience.

31ST YEAR (30–31)

Your thirty-first year is your quintessential four year. It is a year in which you stabilize in all areas of your life. You are becoming

a fully responsible adult and making the commitments necessary to your career and your relationship. Assuming that the
physical and emotional structure of your life is in place, this
might be a good year to start a family or launch a business.

Your thirty-first year will ask you to work hard, to stay
focused on your goals, and to take all the small steps that are
necessary to achieve success. Because so much of your energy
is going outward into the world, it is important that you take
care of your physical body by getting plenty of sleep, eating
well, exercising, and finding some quiet time for rest and
rejuvenation.

Try to find a good rhythm that enables you to be productive without stressing yourself out. Don't be overwhelmed by
all the things that you have to do. Just show up and do what
you can each day. When obstacles arise or things do not flow,
take a break or shift your focus to other tasks. The goal is to
stay in the present and move with life as it unfolds. Move with
the current of the river, not against it. Otherwise, you will tire
yourself out and become discouraged.

As long as you stay in the flow of your life, this is a year
when you can accomplish incredible things without great difficulty. But try to "force" things or to swim against the tide
and you will have a very different experience.

The danger in a four year is that you will over-commit or
bite off more than you can chew and you will wear yourself
out. You will work too many hours and not give yourself time
to rest and recharge. You will take on responsibilities that do
not belong to you and work and family life can become a
burden instead of a joy. If this begins to happen, take time out

and find a way to re-align with the universal energy so that you won't have to struggle so much.

Work without joy is not productive and often leads to lack of energy, depression and other health issues. So keep a watchful eye on yourself. It is easy to become lost in roles and responsibilities and to forget to take care of yourself. And remember, if you are not taking care of yourself, you will not have the energy to take care of others.

32 ND YEAR (31–32)

In your thirty-second year it is important for you to take a break from the daily grind of work roles and responsibilities and step back and see the big picture.

You have spent four years making your vision real and you can see the result of all your discipline and hard work. Your tendency at this point may be to put your head down and keep plugging, but that would be counterproductive. When you are working in a totally focused way, you cannot see the forest for the trees. You get lost in the details. You may waste your time and energy trying to tweak, perfect or control what is already good enough. You might begin to micro-manage and lose the good will of your employees or the cooperation of your partner.

This is a year when you need to expand your consciousness and move beyond old structures and limits. You may go back to school for continued education or training, you might develop a new product or service that builds on what you have already achieved, you might go take a break and go on a much needed vacation, explore a new hobby or interest, or participate in some kind of personal growth workshop or retreat.

This is a time to bring new energy in so that your life does not become predictable or boring. If you don't take some risks this year, if you listen to your fears and turn down opportunities to grow, you may create a prison around you. Your life does not have to be limited to four walls and a roof. You can knock down one of the walls and create a new, more inspired living space.

You can raise the roof and create a second story. Don't be satisfied by what you have done in the past. Without new energy it will become stale and lifeless.

Of course, this is not to suggest that you should abandon what you have built up. But it is time to discover new purpose and meaning in your life. Form must be infused with spirit if it is to be endowed with grace. As Jesus said, "a man does not live by bread alone." Yet that does not mean that he stops eating bread. Instead, he learns to create the bread of life. He aspires to work that brings spiritual nourishment and creative fulfillment.

33RD YEAR (32–33)

By your thirty-third year you have moved beyond limits that were restricting you in your work and personal life. Now you may require new friends and support systems to reinforce your continued growth and individuation. Roles and responsibilities at home and at work may need to shift so that you can be authentic and still fulfill the commitments you have made. This is a year when you and your partner can build a mutually supportive relationship in which you strive for equality and balance in what each of you is giving and receiving from the relationship.

To the extent that you are both able to communicate honestly without shame or blame, and to work together to establish a viable structure for your relationship, this may be a time when you want to publicly celebrate or reaffirm the commitment you have made to each other. Your thirty-third year is a good year to be married or to make other public commitments.

It is also a good year to be actively involved in social groups, religious or civic organizations and in general in the life of your community. If you have children, many of your social activities may be devoted to helping your children connect with other children through sports, arts, or other extra-curricular activities. You may even play a leadership role as a coach, a scoutmaster, or the mentor of a church youth group.

Having taken a year for your personal growth, and learning to say "no" to caretaking roles that burden you and limit your freedom, you are now able to be of service to others in ways that feel good to you.

This is a year when you may have an active social life and communicate with a large number of people. Many people may notice you for the first time and feel attracted to you. Your social persona is intact and more convincing than before because it is more congruent with who you are as a person.

Communicating openly and clearly with your partner, your colleagues and with the public is essential this year.

While it is important to you to be liked by people, you can't please everyone, and you may have to set limits with people who demand an inappropriate amount of your time and energy. Setting healthy boundaries with others will help you to honor yourself and the people you love the most, including your partner and your children, if you have them.

34TH YEAR (33–34)

This is a powerful year of concrete achievement. In a sense, all your ducks are in a row. By now you have developed your talents and gifts and you have gained the self-confidence and self esteem needed for success. Now you can experience how all your hard work will pay off.

This year your creative energy moves into form and production. Your business takes off. Your career as an artist takes a quantum leap. All that you have been working for now becomes manifest and you need to be focused and show up for it.

While this is a year in which your light will shine and you will have great public visibility, you also need to conserve your energy so that you can manage all of the practical activities that are necessary to support your projects. If you don't have time to manage your affairs get some help. Hire a personal assistant or a manager who can help you be prepared.

As is the case with all seven years, the challenge here is to let go of your perfectionism so that your creative energy can flow. Attend to the details but don't get lost in them. You need to see the big picture. You need to be able to get up on stage without worrying that the lights won't work or that the band will forget which notes to play.

Proper team building and preparation can provide you with the ease of heart and mind that you need to show up spontaneously. Learn to breathe and relax. Do the best you can and don't be afraid to make a mistake.

The emotional energy that you bring to your work will overcome any imperfections that arise. If you are inspired and inspire others, your performance does not have to be perfect.

35TH YEAR (34-35)

This is a year when your work and/or family life require some adjustment.

You are coming to the end of your fourth nine year cycle. Last year was a year in which you shined brightly and were very productive. Now the energy has shifted and turned inward. Your cycle has peaked and the time for introspection, adjustment and healing has come.

If you have a family, you may be begin to recognize that you need more time for yourself and more distance from your spouse and children. You may feel that you have already accomplished what you set out to do in your career and you are not sure if you want to continue in the same job or work duties.

This is a year when you can begin to get clear on how your life needs to shift to enable you to heal and come into balance.

The foundation of your life—where and how you live, who you are with, and what you do—is under examination. Your mid-career crisis is approaching.

Beginning the process of looking at your life and seeing what aspects of the foundation still work and what aspects do not is crucial in your thirty-fifth year. In two years, when you move into your thirty-seventh year, it will be time to begin to re-invent your life. Your mid-life crisis will be full blown and you will need the freedom to make changes so that you can continue to grow and individuate as a person.

The danger for you in this year is that you are pulled back into fulfilling old roles and responsibilities that have already served their purpose in your life. That would delay your mid-life crisis and you might feel like you are living in a prison for the next nine years. Of course, it would be a prison of your own making and you can avoid this outcome by paying attention to what needs to shift now.

Don't be surprised if an accident, an illness, or some other unforeseen event forces you to take time to re-evaluate your life. This is a great year to have a break from business as usual, heal and nurture yourself, and cultivate your inner guidance.

36TH YEAR (35-36)

In your thirty-sixth year you will be completing the work of your fourth cycle of life. The fourth cycle is about building the foundation and structure of your career and family life.

By the time you entered your thirty-fourth year, this foundation and structure should have been solid and dependable. Last year, you could have been coming to peace with what you have created, learning from your mistakes, and forgiving yourself and others. Now, as you enter the ninth year of your fourth cycle, you are beginning to detach from what you have created.

All structures can become limiting. What helped to bring solidity and practical grounding for the first seven years of this cycle begins to feel restrictive in year eight and by year nine it must be relinquished.

In this year, that structure may still exist but it is an empty shell because you are withdrawing your energy from it. Without your energy investment and the routine that supports it, the structure is neglected and it starts to fall apart. Your job this year is to detach and let it shift or fall apart.

In your thirty-sixth year you are getting ready to enter your fifth cycle of your life next year. That fifth cycle is characterized by your mid-life crisis. In other words, in the next nine years you are going to experience considerable growth and individuation and the old structure will no longer be able to contain it. Humpty Dumpty will fall off the wall and smash into millions of pieces.

This is the year in which you realize that this shift is inevitable and begin to prepare yourself emotionally for the changes that are going to come.

(36-45)

Mid-Life Crisis Years

37TH YEAR (36-37)

This is a great year to take a sabbatical from work, to travel the globe, go back to school, enroll in a self-improvement program, or to cultivate other new experiences that will expand your perspective. Because this is the first year of your fifth cycle—which brings major growth and change into your life—this year is about expanding your consciousness so that your life does not become routine, predictable and boring. Your previous cycle was all about creating stability in your life. This new nine year cycle is about loosening up the structures of your life so that you have room to grow. It is helpful to embark on new projects that challenge you and engage your creative energy.

As in all one years, you do not know exactly where your life is going and you do not have to know. This is a time to dream, to explore, to take risks. Don't allow yourself to be pressured to hold onto old commitments out of fear or guilt. Recognize that your life is changing. Old structures should have begun dissolving two years ago and last year you should have become detached from the events and circumstances of the old cycle.

Your capacity to move into the chaotic but playful energy of the new cycle is essential to opening your life up to its full creative potential. This is the year to claim your freedom and find a new meaning. purpose and perspective for your life.

38TH YEAR (37–38)

Hopefully you took time last year to have new experiences and to explore new directions for your life. This year you will begin to internalize and integrate these experiences and start to do the research necessary to begin sketching out a plan for the next eight years. You won't be taking the journey in this year, but you will be actively preparing for it, getting the logistics sorted out, organizing and refining your ideas and strategies, and getting help from those who have taken the journey before and can alert you to some of the challenges you will face along the way.

Your quest for information may be a formal one that involves education and training, or it may be an informal one that involves networking and doing research on the internet. Either way, you are digging in and anchoring your vision. Last year you planted the seed, this year you are watering the young plant and weeding the ground around it, and next year it will begin to grow and bloom.

As in all two years, you are not just finding out the outer facts you need to know. You are also checking in with your intuition to be sure that you are moving in a direction that is joyful and fulfilling for you. Both heart and mind must be fully engaged in the process of creation. Next year you will begin to take your new direction out into the world. You will be making new relationships, building alliances, and communicating your vision actively to others. The time that you spend this year getting clear about where you want to go and preparing to take the journey will pay off next year when it is time to act definitely.

39TH YEAR (38-39)

This is a year when you will be actively communicating with people and building alliances that will enable you to implement the vision you have been nurturing for the last two years. You are in the process of opening up the structures of your life to accommodate new psychological growth. This process enables you to be more authentic and true to yourself in the way that you participate in the relationships in your life.

It is inevitable that the changes that are happening for you will have an impact on your current relationship, if you have one. It is essential that you and your partner communicate about the changes that are necessary to allow both of you the time and space to grow as individuals. Honesty is essential as each of you speaks from the heart about what you want and need and you work together to create a common vision for the relationship.

If your partner is in a stable place in life and is not threatened by your growth, s/he can be supportive of you as you actively reach out to others during your thirty-ninth year. If, on the other hand, s/he is threatened by your growth, you may both find that you have to back off from the commitments you have made to each other so that each person is free to find the nurturing and support that s/he needs.

Good communication skills and boundaries will help both of you to take responsibility for your own thoughts, feelings, words and deeds, without criticizing or blaming the other person. If you are going to remain together, you need to find ways to renew the energy in the relationship so that you don't become bored or frustrated with the routines that are in place.

This is a year of expansion for you. You need the freedom to move forward to create work and relationship structures that honor you. It is important for you to think and act outside of the box. Hopefully your partner understands this and can give you the freedom that you need.

If you do not take the time to "grow" the relationship now, one or both of you may become dissatisfied and possibly drawn to other potential partners.

A long term relationship that is not renewed in the thirty-ninth year is likely to fall apart in the forty-fourth year. If you know that now you can take action before it is too late.

On the other hand, if you are not currently in a relationship, your thirty-ninth year is a good year to meet someone who is also experiencing expansion and personal growth and is in alignment with your vision of your life. As you grow and individuate, you spontaneously attract people who share your values, goals and beliefs. Important romantic and career connections often result.

40TH YEAR (39-40)

In your fortieth year, you begin to put into place the new structures that are needed for you to reinvent your life. As a result, this should be a fairly stable and productive year for you. Perhaps you have found ways to breathe new life into your career by taking on more interesting and challenging tasks. Perhaps you and your partner have redefined some of your roles and responsibilities for taking care of children and the home. For example, maybe you quit your job and you are working at home providing childcare while you begin to launch a new business. If you are already in business, perhaps you have begun delegating tasks to others so that you have more time to focus on your personal growth. There are lots of possibilities.

Your mid-life crisis can begin as early as your thirty-sixth year. So you are now four years into it. If you have made the changes that are called for, your life should begin to have a different look and feel than it did at the beginning of this cycle. You should feel that you have moved away from duty and sacrifice and are getting in touch with your passion and purpose. The next three years should see the completion of your mid-life shift during which you have built the foundation for a new, more congruent and authentic life.

If you cannot see this happening, then it is possible that you did not fully heed the call for change when it came four years ago. You may still be holding on to old structures, roles and responsibilities that keep you locked into a lifestyle you find limiting and depressing. If this is the case, big changes may happen for you next year when it becomes impossible for you to betray yourself any longer.

Without bringing in new creative energy, you may feel like you are living in a prison of your own making in your fortieth year. If you don't begin to move beyond those limits this year, you will see the walls of the prison explode in your forty-first year. To make your transition to an expanded life easier begin to lay the groundwork now for your release. Begin thinking and acting outside the box. Be honest and authentic with others. Place emphasis more on your personal growth and cultivate activities that take you out of your comfort zone and allow you to grow. By actively anticipating your mid-life crisis, you can avoid some of the trauma and drama associated with this time of life.

41 ST YEAR (40–41)

This is your quintessential five year. It is the year when it is important for you to get in touch with the psychological and spiritual needs that have brought on your mid-life crisis. Your forty-first year is the mid-point in the cycle of 81 years. It represents a turning point in your life journey as you move from adulthood to maturity. Whereas in the past you may have placed survival and security needs first in the attempt to support yourself and your family, it is now important to address your higher needs to live a life of purpose and meaning. That means it is no longer possible for you to do work that you do not love or live in a relationship with someone you don't love just to keep the status quo. The status quo does not work anymore.

It is time for you to move out of the box you have created in your life and begin to explore new directions. This is a year when you must claim your freedom to expand and explore or pay the price of self-betrayal. The structure that you have created—the roles that you play and the responsibilities that you have taken on —must shift and begin to reflect and support your emerging needs for individuation. You can no longer find meaning just in supporting and taking care of others. You need to learn to care for yourself and give yourself permission to follow your passion and pursue your dreams.

This is the year when honoring yourself is essential in order for you to avoid the drama and trauma that might otherwise be associated with your mid-life crisis. Take a break from your regular routines and duties. Travel, take a sabbatical, go back to school, expand a hobby you love into a part time job. Begin to create the elements that will be needed to re-invent your life. The next three years are crucial in liberating you from limiting roles, exploring new communities and support systems and beginning to come into your creative power as a self-actualized person.

The mid-life crisis can be thought of as a "second birth." The first birth was your physical birth. Now you are experiencing your psychological and spiritual birth. Ideally this happens during the fifth cycle of nine years (ages 36-44) and your forty-first year is the most important year in that cycle for the growth and expansion of your consciousness. If you have not begun to move out of the box of your life during the previous four years, you may begin to feel like a failure (even if the external factors in your life still look good to others). The form appears intact, but you know that it is empty. It no longer satisfies. It is just a shell about to crack open.

Now is a time to begin to live from the inside out. Don't be defined by what you do or how you show up for others. Begin to show up for yourself and pay attention to what you need so that you can begin to live in integrity. Be honest and authentic. Be true to yourself.

Don't be the victim of your own life. Take responsibility. Create a life that is an expression of who you are and gives voice to your most important values and beliefs. This is a time to honor your psychological needs and your spiritual aspirations.

42 ND YEAR (41–42)

Your forty-second year is a time when you need to find social structures that can support your emerging needs for change and transformation. Your last year was a key year in your mid-life crisis and hopefully you began to actively explore new life directions. Perhaps you went back to school, took a sabbatical or changed careers. In some important ways your life shifted and the old family structures may have been revised in order to keep pace with your growth and development. That may mean that you and your spouse had to renegotiate old agreements and make changes in your mutual responsibilities at work or at home.

If you had children in your twenties, you may already anticipate the freedom that comes when the nest is empty and your children go off to work or college. If you had children in your thirties, your children may be more independent now and you may have time to go back to work or school part time.

Regardless of your specific situation, your forty-second year asks you to find new friends and communities that support the changes that you have recently gone through in your life. For example, if you got divorced or separated last year, you might find it helpful to join a men's or woman's group comprised of people experiencing a similar transition. If you stopped drinking, you might find support in the AA community.

The point is that as you open up to new experiences and undergo major life transitions you need to develop new friends and support systems. Being part of a community of people who have similar experiences is essential. You do not have to do all this by yourself. Indeed, trying to go it alone without support decreases your chances of making a successful transition.

Sometimes you try in vain to rely on old friends or family members for support and you are disappointed when they cannot show up for you. They simply do not understand, nor can they support the changes that have happened in your life. You may feel judged or rejected and that just makes everything more difficult for you.

It is always hard to let go of relationships with people who have supported you in the past, but when you see clearly that they cannot be there for you, you must learn to let go. Then you can reach out and find other people who are going through their mid-life crises and you can support each other through the difficult but necessary changes that must be made on the journey to empowerment.

43 RD YEAR (42–43)

In your forty-third year, you will have surrounded yourself with new friends and spiritual communities that support you in stepping into your power and purpose as a unique human being. This year is the apex of your fifth cycle.

It is a time when you are expressing yourself with abundant creativity and self confidence. Others notice you and are uplifted by your example. They see how you are courageously following your heart and expressing your talents and gifts.

This is a year when you will be very engaged in the world. You will become visible to others and as a result may draw not only praise but also criticism. This goes with the territory of empowerment. Not everyone is going to like you. Indeed some people may feel threatened by you because you have given yourself permission to shine and they may see this as selfish or self-indulgent.

Of course, there is a huge difference between self-fulfillment and self-indulgence. The former is the natural result of the individuation process that allows you to be a one-of -a -kind human being with unique talents and gifts. The other suggests that you have somehow risen to notoriety at the expense of others.

Some people will never rise beyond co-dependence and will spend their lives taking care of others or expecting others to take care of them. Those people simply do not self-actualize. Indeed, they hold each other back. They are the ones who are most threatened by people who successfully individuate.

Your responsibility in this embodiment is not to show up as

others expect you to, but to give birth to your creative potential. This is a year when you will be doing just that. Because you are expressing yourself authentically with passion and purpose, you bring abundance into all areas of your life. This is true both energetically and economically. Indeed, the two are intimately connected. By inspiring others energy of all kinds flows back to you.

44TH YEAR (43–44)

If you did not take time in your thirty-fifth year (9 years ago) or in your forty-first year (3 years ago) to consider how the structure of your life needed to shift to enable you to grow and individuate, this is the year when restructuring is unavoidable. Nine years ago change was voluntary. Three years ago it was mandated. If you did not hear the wake up call then, you won't be able to ignore it any longer. Now change is involuntary and may come from the outside through an illness, an accident or a health crisis.

Your mid-life crisis is in full swing and chances are that Humpty Dumpty is no longer sitting on the wall, but has hit the ground and smashed into thousands of pieces, none of which can be salvaged or fit back together.

You can no longer live life on automatic pilot, showing up to take care of others instead of listening to your own needs for growth. This is the year when addictions to work or to drugs and alcohol must be dealt with. They no longer are effective in anesthetizing your pain. Your pain intensifies and must be acknowledged and dealt with.

If the crash has not come yet in your life, it will come soon. Take a step back and look at your life. Take a leave of absence from your job. Enter a twelve step program. Go on a spiritual retreat. Take time to feel your pain, face your self-betrayal and begin to rebuild your life, from the inside out.

If on the other hand, your mid-life crisis has successfully peaked (last year), now is the time to begin to think about how all the changes you have made can be integrated back into a family and social structure that will provide support for your new life. While a seven year period of expansion and experimentation was necessary and liberating for you, you cannot be a heretic or a renegade forever. You must integrate back into the society in which you live. And if old social structures have collapsed, new ones must eventually be created.

45TH YEAR (44-45)

This is the last year of your mid-life crisis years. During the last eight years you have given yourself permission to explore new directions in work and relationship. You have created a more flexible structure that enables you to have the time and the freedom that you need to re-energize and re-invent your life.

This may have involved leaving a career or a marriage or it may have involved shifting your duties and responsibilities in the career or the relationship. As your children grew to be more independent, more time was available for you to explore new horizons.

Now your life looks very different than it looked at the beginning of the cycle. Some people may have judged you for being selfish or self-indulgent because you claimed the freedom you needed to grow, but growth is inevitable and form must expand to contain the necessary growth. The hermit crab must leave the shell that has become too tight and find a larger shell to inhabit.

Now that you have given birth to your gifts and talents and are actively creating your life, you are getting ready to take all that you have learned back into a new more expanded structure of family and community. In your forty-fifth year, you complete your individual journey and begin to detach from the activities of the last eight years.

You enter the stage of chrysalis in which you will eventually be reborn not just as an individual who has learned to be true to himself, but as a responsible member of a community. That is what will happen in the next nine year cycle.

In this ninth year of the present cycle, you no longer need to push the envelope. You can relax and sink in. You can begin to get clear on what you have to offer to the world that you live in.

(45-54)

Stable Mid-Life Years

46TH YEAR (45-46)

In your forty-sixth year you need to create new friendships and participate in groups and communities where you feel accepted and supported and where your needs for belonging can be met. With your mid-life crisis peaking in your forty-first year (40-41) you began to seek new friends and social groupings in your forty-second year (41-42). By now you have left the old structures behind and you are ready to create a whole new social structure for your life. Perhaps your children are now grown. Perhaps you have divorced or separated. By now you realize that you are not the same person that you were when you first married and/or began to raise a family.

The social mask that you used to wear has come off. The ways in which you engaged superficially with others in the past are no longer satisfying. Now you need real connection with people who are honest and authentic with you. Building a new community can be challenging but it is also exciting. You will have to come out of your shell and let yourself be seen. You will have to reach out and ask for what you want.

Whereas in the past you may have built a social persona to support your role as a spouse, a parent or a member of your church, you are now faced with the challenge of expressing yourself more transparently as a unique individual with needs for social acceptance and belonging. Your last cycle of 9 years brought many changes as you went through your mid-life crisis. Your sense of your own identity was no doubt transformed as well. You are now a more awakened and conscious human being. As a result you are more clear about what you need and what you have to give to others. Discovering a community that is a fit for your more authentic, revealed self is the work of the next nine year cycle in your life.

47TH YEAR (46–47)

In your forty-seventh year you continue your search for a new social network of friends and family who can support you on your journey. Even if you do not yet know exactly where you "fit in," you do know where you do "not fit in."

You know that you are no longer satisfied by superficial connections. You are looking for connections that are deeper and more soulful.

Consequently, you look for friends who have a certain psychological depth and can understand the changes that have happened in your consciousness and your life during the last 10 years. Just as no book can be judged by its cover, no human being can be understood from the roles that they play at home or at work. So much has changed in the way your life looks and feels, only a person who has undergone similar transformation can hold the space for you when you are challenged in life. In the same manner, your ability to hold the space for others deepens as you go through major life transitions such as divorce, career change, health crises, or children leaving the nest to go off to school or work.

Experience always makes you stronger and more determined to be who you are. Self betrayal at this time of life is no longer an option. Being a caretaker whose life is defined by meeting the needs of others no longer satisfies. Younger people who are stuck in codependent or abusive relationships may admire the freedom you have claimed in your life and be drawn to you. You are in a unique position to help others learn to move out of sacrifice and self betrayal.

Moreover, by being a member of a community of authentic adults who are drawn to give back to others, you may have opportunities to serve that feel satisfying to you. The key is that now you are giving because you want to and know how to, not because you have to. You are not seeking social approval, but rather helping to extend the web of caring and support to others who need it.

Yet this is not a year when you have to be active in service or community activities. Rather, it is a year in which you begin to become clear about what you need from a community and what you have to give in return. It may be that last year you began to explore many different options for social connection and this year you are beginning to understand which ones satisfy the most. Your forty-seventh year is a time when you begin to find clarity and a direction in your search for community in your life.

48TH YEAR (47–48)

In your forty-eighth year you have a very active social life and are engaged in building many new supportive relationships with people who understand you and share your values and interests. Because you are so visible, it is likely that you may draw a romantic relationship into your life if you do not already have one.

It is likely that you and your partner belong to the same group and, if so, your relationship will have a public as well as a private side. Both of you may become very conscious of how you look to the outside world and do your utmost to present a harmonious image to others. To the extent that you both have become more clear about who you are and what you want this public image may not be misleading. It may reflect the actual level of trust and intimacy you have together. If that is not the case, the image you present to the world may be yet another mask that sooner or later will fall away. Most romantic bubbles do burst and when they do so publicly they can be embarrassing if not humiliating.

To avoid setting yourself up for disappointment, it is important that the private aspect of your relationship be nurtured through honest communication, frequent sharing and acceptance of differences. Real intimacy cannot be destroyed even if the public persona is tarnished. Two people who are committed to each other will find a way to overcome any obstacles in their path.

On the positive side, this is a year when you could receive praise and attention as an authentic role model for other couples. Because you learn how to find a balance between the private and public aspects of the relationship you can be active together in your community without sacrificing the ongoing trust and intimacy that you share.

49TH YEAR (48–49)

In your forty-ninth year, you are actively developing new extended families, social structures and organizations that can meet your own needs and the needs of others whom you care about.

This is a year when you can fully express your passionate commitment to building community. You will join with others and work very hard to implement your shared vision. In addition, your career will be thriving and you will be very visible in your community.

Your mid-life crisis was all about re-creating the structure of your life so that it was more congruent with who you are. This meant letting go of family and social roles that pleased others, reinforced your co-dependence and ultimately led to self-betrayal. Having relinquished old social structures that no longer worked in your life, you were ready to build new ones that reflected all the growth that occurred in your mid-life years.

By now you are no longer afraid of disappointing others. You know that you are no longer living your life to please or win the approval of other people.

Your life is now about self-empowerment and the support of others to create an empowered life. You are no longer willing to be a victim or to stay in co-dependent relationships or in groups where you have to conform to rigid norms.

While in the past other people defined and related to you based on the work that you did or the roles that you played, now they relate to you as an authentic person who lives from the inside out and cannot be boxed in or defined by external roles. Indeed, they know that you are a force to be reckoned with.

You live with passionate intensity. You are willing to do whatever needs to be done to move things forward. You chop wood, carry water, show up at meetings, inspire and manage others. You get people to buy into the vision and actively support the organizations to which you are committed.

You have learned to live without guilt for pursuing your dreams and your passions. You are able to move forward, even when other people judge you and don't understand. And when the support of your old friends falls away you make new friends and alliances.

Your forty-ninth year is a time of great practical achievement for you. It is probably one of the most productive years of your life. This is a year when you have tremendous visibility and are well respected and appreciated in your community. Your hard work pays off with measurable results and others directly benefit from your service.

50TH YEAR (49–50)

The new communities you have been developing in the last four years support you in staying outside of the box, being true to yourself and living an authentic life. This is a year when expansion of consciousness is also necessary.

After an intensive year working hard in your career and building community around you, it will be time for you to take a step back and look at what you have accomplished. It is important not to lose yourself in work and routines or you will not see what needs to shift in order for your projects to continue to grow. Taking a year to travel or study what others are doing can help you get needed perspective on your work and help you bring new energy and insight to bear on it.

If, on the other hand, you have not honored the emerging psychological and spiritual needs of your mid-life crisis, your fiftieth year may be a difficult one. You may still be trying to live your life to please others and keep the old social structures in place. The problem is that those roles, responsibilities, and routines no longer work. Others are no longer pleased. They feel that you are not showing up for them, perhaps because they know that you are just going through the motions and that your heart is not in it anymore.

If this is the case, it will be time now for you to stop pretending to be someone you are no longer. This is a year when you must stop the charade. Come back into your heart. Get clear on what you need and want. Be honest and ask others for the freedom you need to individuate.

It is better to risk disappointing others than it is to live in self-betrayal. Self-betrayal inevitably leads to the betrayal of others. It is just a matter of time. Save yourself and others that future trauma and make the courageous choice to honor yourself right now. In the end, it is the best gift that you can give to the people who share your life.

51ST YEAR (50–51)

This is your quintessential sixth year. It is a year that celebrates the success of the social networks you have built and the services you have offered to the people in your community who need assistance and support.

Building organizations that are responsive to the needs of the people they serve is never easy. It requires a deep level of compassion and an ability to communicate with diverse groups of people, all of whom have their unique needs and perspectives. Your ability to listen to what people need and build consensus pays off this year as you see the organizations you have supported or developed prospering and fulfilling their purpose.

Personally, you have found your place in the world. You feel that you can be yourself authentically even in the public arena and people appreciate and respect you. Whether you are a leader or a follower, people know that they can count on you to show up for them. This gives you great credibility.

You may choose to capitalize on your positive reputation by running for political office or assuming a highly visible position of leadership in the community. That is entirely appropriate given the success that you have had. As you become more widely known and ascend to a position of power, you can have an even greater impact on the health and well-being of your community.

Be careful though to make sure that your motives are honorable. Many people who rise to power and privilege take advantage of their positions to benefit themselves, their friends and family, instead of the wider community that they serve. They violate the public trust and may suffer public censure or even humiliation.

Don't go down that road. Don't be selfish or sloppy. Pay careful attention to what you say and do. It is easy for words to be misinterpreted and for motives to be misunderstood. Strive for honesty and transparency in all that you say and do and you will continue to win the public's trust and respect.

52 ND YEAR (51–52)

As was the case last year, your creative self expression naturally leads you into community with others. This is a year when you will be very visible expressing your talents and gifts on the public stage.

Whereas in the past you may have been afraid to express yourself authentically for fear of criticism or rejection, now you know that you have to have the courage to be yourself, even if others do not like what you have to share.

While in your last cycle (at age 43, for example) you may have developed the confidence to put your creative work out there, you may have done so in a way that was rebellious, brash or in-your face. While some people may have been attracted to this, others were probably turned off and may have dismissed you as self-indulgent, egotistical or solipsistic. By now you have mellowed and are more convivial in your self expression. As a result you speak more to the universal themes and desires of people and as a result your work finds a wider audience.

Because you no longer feel that you have to prove your self-worth or seek the approval of others, your harsh edge softens and people more easily accept you and recognize you as a brother or sister. Instead of trying to shine for yourself alone, or at the expense of others, you now shine as person who inspires and empowers others to believe in themselves.

In this important year of self expression and public visibility you are establishing the platform on which you will ascend into the fullness of your creative power and prominence in your sixtieth and sixty-first years of life.

53 RD YEAR (52–53)

For the last five years of your life you have been very involved creating new extended families, social networks and communities that address your needs for social support and belonging. You have successfully incorporated into your life the growth and individuation that occurred during your mid-life crisis.

Now, most of that work is done and it is time for your energy to begin to turn inward again. As in all eight years, this is a year to take time for the healing, forgiveness, and psychological adjustment that are necessary to bring greater balance into your life.

One of the adjustments that you will need to make is coming to terms with the changes that are taking place in your physical body as you go through menopause and the change of life. Now you will have to learn to listen to what your body needs and take good care of yourself. You may have to shift your expectations of yourself, slow down, deal more consciously with stress, and learn to invest your energy wisely. Aging does not have to be a negative experience if you accept it and adjust to your changing needs.

The challenges come when you don't accept the change of life and are trying to prove to yourself and others that you are still thirty years younger. Attempts to improve the exterior of your body (how you look) though elective cosmetic surgery do not necessarily address your need for greater health and balance in your life (how you feel). If you work on taking care of yourself by eating well, exercising, and reducing the amount of stress in your life, you will feel better and, as a result, look better. Positive changes happen from the inside out, not from the outside in.

Your job in your fifty-third year is not to make a new mask or obsess on your appearance, but to address any health issues you have by changing old destructive habits of consumption, simplifying your life, and adopting a healthy lifestyle. It is also important to cultivate a positive attitude and to surround yourself with a network of friends who are also learning to live in a healthy and empowered way.

54TH YEAR (53-54)

This is the last year of your sixth cycle. In the last eight years you have found a way to be authentically present in your family and your community. You have made new friendships and found new groups of people who support you in your growth, and you have found ways to give back to others, sharing what you have learned from the years of your mid-life crisis. You have become visible to others and have taken on responsibilities that you enjoy fulfilling. You have created a solid foundation on which you will build consistently, as you come into your full creative power in the next nine years.

This is a year when you may find yourself pulling back from some of your social commitments as you make space for yourself to nurture the strong creative energies that have been seeded during this cycle. You may need time in silence or in nature. You may go on a spiritual retreat. This year you are entering the womb that will birth you into the most creative and productive years of your life.

Don't be afraid to give yourself the time and the space that you need. Be glad for the social connections you have cultivated. They will be very helpful for you in the future. But let people know that you need some time for yourself. Tell them you are working on some wonderful creative projects that need your time and attention. They will understand.

Even if you are not feeling creative right now, you still need the time to be present and sink in. It is important to detach and not be distracted by outside energies and expectations. Let the ground lie fallow so that the nutrients in the soil can be renewed. Then, when the time for planting comes, the crop will be abundant.

(54-63)

Self-Actualization Years

55TH YEAR (54-55)

By the time you enter your fifty-fifth year, your mid-life crisis is complete. You have surrendered old family and social support systems, built new friendships and created new spiritual families where you can be yourself authentically. You now trust yourself and feel ready to actively express your talents and gifts freely in the world.

In this year, you will take new risks and explore new avenues of self expression. You will learn to trust your own creative process and to feel the support of the universe behind you as you have the courage and the confidence to be yourself. The next nine years will be a cycle of mastery and creative fulfillment for you. You will do what you love to do. You will live in joy, trust and spontaneity. In this nine year cycle your life purpose will be fulfilled.

In the beginning, don't be surprised if old fears of failure come up and test you. Now you have the strength to walk through those fears. You aren't going to hold yourself back or try to show up to please others. Those days of self-betrayal are over. Now that you are committed to being yourself you cannot fail. So "feel the fear and do it anyway." Know that the universe supports you in individuating and expressing your unique talents and gifts in the world.

As in all one years, please remember this is not a time to put pressure on yourself. Success will come naturally in its own time and place. This is a year to experiment, try new approaches, nurture the vision, and be intuitively with the creative projects that will take shape during the next two years. Your patience and gentleness with yourself will do more than anything else to nurture the inner vision and give it the period of gestation that it needs to have a timely and successful birth into the world.

56TH YEAR (55–56)

In this year you become clear about who you are and how and what you want to share with others. You are in touch with both thoughts and feelings. You are listening not just to your head, but also to your heart. You have let go of the need of trying to please others and are feeling free and empowered to be yourself. That means accepting how you are different from others and giving yourself permission to express yourself honestly and authentically. This is a year when you will know and experience yourself from the inside out and begin preparation for a new more authentic expression of yourself in the world.

Don't be surprised if the creative project that is now incubating and finding direction looks very different from anything that you have done in the past.

In some respects it may be more simple and compelling. You have a new confidence in your creative ability and you are not afraid to take a risk. You also have a much better idea of what speaks to people's hearts and you don't hesitate to take time doing the necessary research, study and preparation that the new work requires.

In your fifty-sixth year you are getting ready to launch the work that will be the centerpiece of your creative life. Next year and for the next five years you will see that work shared and celebrated by others. These years will be your peak years of self-actualization when your greatest creative achievements take place.

57TH YEAR (56–57)

Your fifty-seventh year is a time when you begin to share with others the creative projects that you have been developing during the last two years. Now people begin to see what you have been up to and they are excited to hear more about it. Your creative work flourishes in your fifty-seventh year.

This is also one of the best years for partnership or marriage and it is in general a time when you enjoy many successful relationships with others. By now you have developed the capacity to communicate honestly and you are clear about what you need and want in a partnership. You have moved beyond roles and responsibilities that are limiting to you and you are able to live in a way that is true to yourself, no longer attempting to please others or win their approval.

You have the courage and freedom to be yourself and the wisdom to allow others to be as they are. The days of co-dependent relationships are over. Now you know and so does your partner that you have no choice other than to be yourself and tell the truth about your experience. This is a year when you (either with or without your partner) may be a teacher, leader, facilitator or role model showing others how to live authentically in partnership with others. You exhibit great self-confidence that inspires others and gives them hope that they too can be successful in cultivating fulfilling relationships with others.

When both people in a relationship are empowered and free to be themselves their relationship embodies the kind of equality and mutual respect that enables them to thrive and accomplish their creative goals, both alone and together.

The capacity to support and collaborate with the partner makes many things possible that could not have happened if each person was functioning alone. Together you and your partner learn to surrender to a deeper creative impulse that enables you to experience abundance and prosperity in all aspects of your lives.

58 TH YEAR (57-58)

In your fifty-eighth year you have stabilized in your new cycle. You are doing work that you love and that creatively expresses who you are. You have many fulfilling relationships with others.

You have found a structure for your life that supports your creative work and your relationships and helps you to move with the flow of the universe. This is a year of genuine abundance because the creative energy that you put out naturally brings back the resources that you need to live and thrive. Similarly, the commitments that you make feel natural. They do not burden you or put pressure on you to perform or produce. You work with joy and relate to others in a supportive and empowering way. You have finally created a life that flows easily, following its own current, like a river moving toward the sea. The goal and the journey are one and the same. So with every step you take you can feel satisfaction, because you know that the destination will be reached in due time.

Because you have learned to trust yourself and do whatever needs to be done without complaining, life lives itself. You don't have to push the river. You chop wood, carry water, show up when and how you are needed and things move forward without great difficulty. Even when the storms of life arrive, you weather them patiently, knowing that all storms will pass and dissolve into moments of peace and tranquility. Because you learn to live in trust and gratitude, grace unfolds in your life.

In your fifty-eighth year, your creativity and life purpose are manifest. Like a poem or a painting in the making, your creative genius flows forth into the world. Your gifts are given freely and received with appreciation.

59TH YEAR (58–59)

If you succeeded in re-inventing your life during your mid-life crisis, this will be a watershed year for you. You will have learned to be honest and authentic with others and to find friends and communities that support you in being true to yourself.

As a result, this is a year when you can really shine. People can see your self confidence and willingness to be out there expressing who you are. All your creative energies are engaged and you are modeling for others what it means to be a self-actualized human being.

This is a year of great personal freedom to create, travel and expand your consciousness. Nothing can hold you back. You have the momentum of a successful mid-life crisis behind you and the wind is at your back. All the time you spent on personal growth, risk taking and spiritual exploration is paying off. You are becoming fully and completely yourself.

A great teacher is not just someone who knows his subject matter. A great teacher models what s/he is teaching. Because you have done your own experiential learning, what you share with others as a leader, a teacher, or a guide inspires and uplifts them. In you they sense their own freedom to self-actualize.

This is a year when you may have a great impact on others, encouraging them to trust their creative energies and commit to their own personal growth and development.

60TH YEAR (59–60)

This is the year in which you will receive recognition from your community for your leadership and creative contributions. Your success in building community around you begins to pay off as you become increasingly visible and others begin to let you know how you have inspired them. Last year, this year and next year (your sixty-first year) will be watershed years for you in terms of your public notoriety and success. You will be shining all of your light out in the world and others will see it and celebrate it. You will be a strong mentor, teacher, and leader for others.

This is not a year to hold back. It is a year to step forward and share authentically with others. Whether you shine in politics, in your church or synagogue, in community service, the arts or athletics, your skills and talents will not go unnoticed. You will have the public venues you need to express yourself confidently and creatively.

61 ST YEAR (60–61)

This is your quintessential seven year. It is the year in which you come into the fullness of your creative power and public visibility. You express your talents and gifts with a confidence and a reach that surpass anything you have known in your life so far. This is your mastery year.

Opportunities for creative expression spontaneously arise and you walk fearlessly through all of the open doors, trusting the universe to support you. You experience abundance and prosperity on all levels.

You are a role model inspiring others to believe in themselves and to trust their talents and gifts. This is a year in your life when you experience not only the joy and fulfillment of your creative process but also the positive impact you have on the community in which you live.

As long as you believe in yourself, there are no limits on what you can accomplish this year. You are living in harmony with the universal supply and grace is operating fully in your life.

62 ND YEAR (61–62)

Last year was a time when you were able to ride the wave all the way in to the shore. It was a year in which you shined in all your creative intensity and people expressed their gratitude and appreciation to you. Your sixty-second year may seem to be somewhat of an anti-climax. The wave eventually crashes on the beach and the exhilarating ride is over. This is a year when you may find that you don't have as much energy to be expressing yourself in public. As in all eight years, this is a year when your energy begins to turn inward and you start to internalize what you have experienced in the last five active years of your cycle.

In your sixty-second year, you begin to see the consequences of your actions. Your birds come home to roost and you must live with them. There may be a need to make amends with people, to forgive yourself and others, to accept and learn from your mistakes.

There may be a health crisis to weather. You may need to find healing practitioners and therapists who can help you through this time of adjustment. This is a year for healing and bringing balance back into your life. Your energy has been moving outward for five years. Your cup is almost empty. There isn't much left to give.

In this year, you begin to fill your cup again. The balance shifts from giving to receiving, from helping others to receiving help.

Your cooperating in the healing and re-balancing process is essential. If you are still out there trying to catch the next wave you are not listening to what your body, mind and soul need. Stop trying to be superman or woman. It won't work any more.

Pull your energy in and conserve it. Take good care of yourself. Allow yourself to integrate and reconcile your experience. Start moving into the detachment that will be required of you during the next two years.

63RD YEAR (62-63)

This is the last year of your seventh cycle. During the last eight years you have shined as never before in your life. People have been inspired by your creativity and leadership and you have been much appreciated. But all good things come to an end. Periods of intensive creativity must be followed by periods of rest, balancing, and rejuvenation. Last year and this year are times when your energy is again being withdrawn from the world and you are beginning to turn inward. This is entirely appropriate.

Last year you may have experienced a health crisis that underscored your need for healing and re-balancing. This year you will begin to detach from all that you have been doing for the last eight years. While you clearly identify with what you have done confidently and enthusiastically, it is now time to withdraw the identification. You are not what you do. You are greater than that. Indeed, all your self worth is present even though you are doing nothing and going nowhere.

It may be difficult for you to sit still when you are so used to being out there. But it is necessary. You have given abundantly to others and now it is time to rest, nurture yourself, and fill your cup.

(63-72)

Adjustment/Retirement Years

64TH YEAR (63-64)

Your eighth cycle of nine years is a time when many adjustments need to be made. You are moving out of your time of peak creativity and achievement into a period of time in which your energy turns inward and you begin to think about retirement. During these next nine years, a health crisis may arise that requires you to make changes in your lifestyle or you may voluntarily begin to simplify your life, taking some of the pressure off so that you can take better care of your body.

As in all one years, your sixty-fourth year is a time of new beginnings and new experiences. You will experiment and begin to cultivate a vision of what your life will look life in the next nine years. Hopefully, you have begun to detach from the activities of the previous cycle so that you have more time to explore new interests and directions.

This is not a year in which you need to be making commitments or actively engaging with the world. It is a year in which you ask "What's next for me? How do I want to spend the next few years of my life? Where do I want to live? What do I want to spend my time doing?"

You may decide to explore hobbies or interests that you have put on the back burner, because you have not had time to pursue them in the past. Now you begin to make time for the activities that give you pleasure and bring greater peace into your life. This year and for the next nine years, it is time to smell the roses, to enjoy the simple pleasures of life, and to give your aging body the attention it needs so that you can stay healthy.

65TH YEAR (64–65)

Your sixty-fifth year is a time for psychological adjustment. You begin to think and feel about yourself differently as your body ages and your focus turns inward. You realize that tasks that you used to accomplish automatically now require conscious attention. As your body ages, you need to make space for self-care and you need to slow down so that you have the time you need to take care of your health and that of your partner, if you have one.

Slowing down is harder for some people than it is for others. Some people refuse to see the writing on the wall and they push themselves beyond their capacities. That kind of denial of the aging process is bound to lead to a health crisis at some time during this nine year cycle.

If you are wise, you begin to understand and tune in to how your lifestyle needs to change to make it easier for you to age gracefully. In your sixty-fifth year, you begin making plans for retirement. You do research on where and how you want to live. You begin collecting all of the information you need to make good decisions about the future.

While you may not actively make changes in your lifestyle this year, you will be preparing to make those choices next year. You may prepare by doing research on the internet, or by taking a class on travel, financial management, or real estate investment.

In your sixty-fifth year you find clarity and direction about the next seven years of your life. You make a retirement plan that you will begin to act on with energy and enthusiasm next year.

66TH YEAR (65-66)

In your sixty-sixth year you begin to actively communicate with others about your retirement plans and you start acting on those plans. You may travel to look at real estate in retirement locations that interest you. You may purchase a condo or a home.

If you do not have a partner, this is a time when you may attract a partner into your life who shares your dreams and visions of retirement. If you already have a partner, this is a year when you will need to communicate honestly with your partner so that you can ensure that you are on the same page regarding future plans about how and where you want to live together.

Having come out of a period of intense activity in the world you and your partner may not have taken sufficient time to nurture your relationship and communicate your needs and desires. If that is the case, this is the year when you must take the time to do so. Hopefully, last year you collaborated on planning activities and this year you may travel together or work together to make lifestyle choices that you both agree need to be made.

Growing old together without the structure and the cohesion of work and parenting roles is a new experience for both of you. If you are going to continue your journey together, you may have to redefine what it looks and feels like. Taking the time to do this is crucial and will help you both find an authentic way to re-commit to the relationship.

The sixty-sixth year is a time of death and rebirth for a partnership. It is a time when people can no longer rely on old roles and responsibilities to keep them together. They need to meet each other anew and find a deeper intimacy in order for the relationship to be nurtured and sustained through the last years of life.

67TH YEAR (66-67)

If you have not already done so, your sixty-seventh year is a good year to retire from your job, downsize your living situation, and simplify your life. If you do continue to work, try to cut back your hours and do work that is emotionally satisfying and energizing. It is important to stay active physically and to take good care of your health so that you have a good quality of life. Try to consolidate your resources so that you are free to travel and explore new interests and activities in the coming years.

The danger in your sixty-seventh year is that you continue to work hard in your career and push yourself to take on responsibilities that you should be delegating to others. By now you should have made a plan to take some of the pressure off yourself and begin creating a gentler, more leisurely life. While the fear of "not having anything to do" and being bored and restless may arise, it must be faced honestly.

This eighth nine year cycle requires a shift from living an outwardly engaged life to living an inwardly engaged life. That means having time to look at who you are and to cultivate a spiritual perspective. If you are a person who has to stay busy, this may be a hard transition for you to make. However, it is a necessary one. If you do not slow down and make the transition to a gentler, less stressful and more introspective life, you will push the envelope and bring on a health crisis in your seventy-first year.

This is a year to actively implement your retirement plans. It is not a year to try to keep the old structures and responsibilities of your life in place. They should have begun to shift in your sixty-second and sixty-third year, leaving you free to begin creating a different kind of life when the present nine year cycle began in your sixty-fourth year.

68TH YEAR (67-68)

Hopefully by the time you reach your sixty-eighth year you will have implemented your retirement plan and established a solid structure for your new life. If this is the case, your sixty-eighth year can be a year in which you expand your life through travel, education, cultural activities, or spiritual practices. As in all five years, this year is about moving out of the box and bringing more outside stimulation and perspective into your life.

If on the other hand, you have not taken the time for personal growth and development during the two previous nine year cycles, this year may require you to take the time for yourself. You can ignore your psychological needs for growth only so long in your life. When growth is not voluntary, the universe steps in to assist the soul in creating the space it needs for self-transformation.

This is a year when you must take some risks, depart from your routines, and move beyond your comfort zones so that you can grow as a person.

While the retirement years are meant to be a time to slow down and smell the roses, they do not have to be boring. Last year routines were important. They helped you to anchor in your retirement plans. But this is a more active year.

It is a time when you need to reach out and open to new experiences that can enrich your life. You can do this by traveling abroad, participating in a class or elder hostel program, volunteering your time at a local hospice or soup kitchen, learning to play tennis or golf, singing in your church chorus, starting a new hobby. etc. The important thing is not to be too passive and allow your life to become boring and predictable. Otherwise, it may seem that the structure you have created for your retirement years is starting to close in around you.

69th YEAR (68–69)

Your sixty-ninth year is all about building community around you. If you began to reach out and take some risks last year, you have no doubt made new connections and friends with people who share your interests and lifestyle choices. Even as you get older, you need social networks that meet your need for emotional support, connection and belonging.

Your extended family of children, grandchildren, and close friends provides an important context for your life. Yet you have moved beyond your career and child raising years and you need to build new communities of peers to share your life. Participating in social, educational and religious organizations that offer programs for mature adults can be important ways to build community. You also may find that you make wonderful connections with people through volunteering and service work in your community.

This is a year when the natural flow of your life supports social engagement, whatever that looks like to you. Each person has his or her own needs and desires when it comes to the social arena. However, last year, this year and next year are all times in the cycle when you are supported in interacting with others. Isolating and turning inward would not be appropriate now.

70TH YEAR (69–70)

Your seventieth year offers you yet another opportunity to shine as a creative, self-confident human being. While you may no longer have the visibility that comes from a full fledged career, expressing your creativity and sharing what you love with others is still very important. Opportunities to share your knowledge and experience with the next generation may come through volunteer work or teaching a master class.

The idea here is to keep your creative juices flowing and to stay engaged with life. The goal is not to go back to work or to make commitments that would be burdensome to you. In this case, less is better than more. Be sure to prioritize your opportunities to share so that you choose the ones that have the most joy for you and the most impact on others.

This is a year of active creative expression within the context of your retirement years, which inevitably involve some degree of detachment from the affairs of the world. As a result, your seventieth year should not be an attempt to re-identify with your public image or persona. That would interfere with the adjustment that you are making to a gentler and more leisurely life.

The rule for this year is "do it if it is fun and joyful." Don't do it out of duty or nostalgia for the past when you were in the limelight. You don't need to seek adulation or approval any more. You just need to keep sharing your enthusiasm and your joy.

71ST YEAR (70–71)

Your seventy-first year is your quintessential eight year. Again you have moved past the peak of your cycle and your energy is turning inward.

This is the year when you get in touch with the essential lessons of this cycle as well as those of your overall life. In that sense, you begin to come to terms with your karma and see the consequences of the choices that you have made in the past. You reap the results of the seeds that you have sown in your physical body, in your relationships and family life, and in your career.

You may experience a serious illness or health crisis. Guilt may arise about past actions and you may need to make amends and forgive yourself and others. You may struggle because your career has ended and you do not have a vehicle for creative expression in your life.

The keywords for this year and for eight years in general are healing, balancing, forgiving and reconciling. In your seventy-first year these are not optional or part time activities. They require your full time focus and attention. In order to move into the detachment and relinquishment that will be asked of you next year and for the following nine years of the next cycle, you need to devote this year to resolving inner conflict, overcoming guilt or regret, and coming to peace within your heart and mind.

Any spiritual practice that helps you to accomplish these goals is an appropriate use of your time and energy in this year. Moreover, don't be afraid to ask for help from skilled practitioners who can help you heal physically, emotionally, mentally and spiritually. The time you spend coming to peace this year will have a profound effect on the rest of your life.

72 ND YEAR (71-72)

This is the last year of your eighth cycle. During the last eight years you have been going through a major period of adjustment, as you deal with health challenges, forgiveness issues, and the need to come to peace with your life.

Now it is time to lay all that to rest. Now it is time for you to accept the healing that has come and sink into your essence.

Each person must find his core self, which is innocent and cannot be wounded. That pure essence is within your heart of hearts and it is there that you are called to find communion.

When you understand that you have done the best you can, when you know that your mistakes and trespasses can be forgiven, then you can relax and sink into that wholeness within you that is not stained or troubled by the affairs of this world. There you can abide and know that you are accepted and loved.

As in all nine years, this is a year of completion and detachment. Once you have learned the lessons that life has brought, you can begin to forgive and let go of the past. That relinquishment enables you to come into the present moment with greater intensity.

During your next cycle of nine years, you will be asked to continue to detach from the drama of your life. You will no longer live with regrets about the past or preoccupation with the future. You will learn to be present and welcome each day and each moment as it unfolds in your life.

(72-81)

Wisdom Years

73 RD YEAR (72-73)

Your seventy-third year is a time of spiritual awakening. This is the first year of your ninth cycle of life, which is all about detaching from the daily struggles and drama of life and coming into the present moment.

This is a year when you can delight in taking time by yourself to meditate and commune with your own experience. For years you have invested in external activities and relationships. Now it is time to go within and to cultivate the relationship with yourself. When you come into the silence of your heart, you realize that everything that you need is there. This is your core or essential self. This is the place where unconditional love and acceptance abide. As you commune with the core self, you feel connected to all beings and all things. In this sense you do not experience your aloneness as a state of being separate from others but as a state that is inclusive of all. Now you are experiencing the epiphany that comes from the discovery of "all in one" and "one in all."

As in all one years, this is a year when you are opening up to new experiences and new directions. You may go on a pilgrimage or extended spiritual retreat. You may travel to or live in a place that is peaceful and nurturing to you. You may start to meditate or do some other spiritual practice that helps you stay in the present moment. The outward form that your life takes is not as important as the content, which is all about detaching from the drama and centering in the heart.

74TH YEAR (73–74)

Your seventy-fourth year is a year of profound introspection. In the previous year, you may have moved to a new place or made changes in your lifestyle that gave you more time alone and in silence.

This is the year when going into the silence will bring a deeper connection to your core self. With the help of meditation and other tools, you may develop the ability to be the witness of your thoughts and emotions. Being the witness helps you detach from the ups and downs of life and anchor in something deeper and more eternal.

As in all two years, this is a year of study and preparation for the activity that will happen in this cycle. Next year you may be more actively sharing and communicating with others the insights you have gained this year and the year before.

Psychologically, this year corresponds to the synergy that

happens in the psyche as the shadow is integrated, resulting in greater psychological wholeness.

As opposites are accepted and integrated, there is less experience of duality. Mind and heart are no longer at odds as they were before. What you think and how you feel harmonize, so that choices can be made spontaneously and without effort.

75TH YEAR (74–75)

Your seventy-fifth year is a time when you will be actively communicating with others the insights you have gained during the last two years. You will find that your life is able to flow naturally between time in silence and time sharing with others. You will actively follow your inner guidance and make choices and decisions without deliberation or effort.

If you have a partner, your seventy-fifth year can be a watershed year for your relationship. You and your partner can come together with even greater trust, respect and intimacy as you both begin to detach from the drama and sink into your core self. Now you can both be the witness of life as it unfolds.

If you don't have a partner, your seventy-fifth year may bring in a new, mature relationship with a partner who shares your spiritual values and provides you with a pathway to greater self-acceptance and understanding.

Your time in the crucible of relationship has brought wisdom and clarity that others appreciate. You are now an elder and a wisdom keeper who can bring spiritual guidance and insights to others.

This may also be a year when you detach from a relationship that has run its course and is now complete. This will be easier if you can do so with a sense of gratitude for the time shared, the gifts received, and the lessons learned together.

76TH YEAR (75–76)

In your seventy-sixth year you begin to feel a sense of completion in your career and family life. You have seen the fruits of your labors and have stepped back to allow your children and other younger people build on what you have accomplished. You have been able to detach from the demands and responsibilities of the world and cultivate a leisurely life that keeps you active without creating stress or anxiety.

In truth, there is nothing that you need to do any more. Your life is no longer about labor and achievement. It is about enjoying the activities of the day, whatever they may be, and taking time to smell the roses. If work is still important, you may find volunteer work a day or two a week so that your mind stays active and you still feel you are making a contribution to the world in which you live.

Doing simple chores around the house or working in the garden can help to keep you active and focused. But they really serve no other purpose. You could easily pass these responsibilities onto others or pay someone else to handle them for you. You choose to do them only because you find them rewarding.

It is important for you to create a rhythm and routine in your life that enable you to get exercise and proper sleep, to eat well and to attend to your health needs. The older you get, the more basic your life becomes. That is not necessarily tragic. A simple life is a life free of stress and can bring a sense of quiet dignity and fulfillment.

77TH YEAR (76-77)

Your seventy-seventh year is a year of expansion and growth. Last year you worked on establishing a simple rhythm and routine that helped you to stay focused and grounded. This year, if your health allows, it is time to open things up a bit.

As in all five years, your seventy-seventh year supports activities like travel, learning, and personal growth. This is a great year to go on an extended spiritual retreat or to have an experience that inspires you or brings greater meaning into your life.

A year of expansion in which you vary your routines and think outside of the box helps to keep your life interesting. Activities that engage your creativity are optimal this year. You still have a lot to contribute both to your peers and to the younger generation. But you need to go at your own pace and take the pressure off. This is not about "having to do" anything. It is about "wanting to do it" and doing it in a way that is not stressful to you.

As we are told in Ecclesiastes: "for every time there is a season." This is a time and a season for caring for yourself and cultivating activities that are fun to do and that inspire you. It is a time to learn new things you never had time for or to travel to places you always wanted to visit. Rest if you need to rest. Be active in gentle ways that rejuvenate. Taste and explore new activities that create balance in your life. In short, be as creative as you can, follow your own natural rhythms, and continue to detach from anything that brings stress or anxiety into your life.

78TH YEAR (77-78)

Your seventy-eighth year brings yet another opportunity to build your social network and to create an active sense of community in your life. It is wonderful if you can lead or participate in shared activities such as group meditation or yoga, painting or drawing classes, group outings to concerts or theatrical performances, and similar events.

While your experience of aloneness may be deepening as you detach from the world during this cycle, it is important to stay connected to family and friends who accept you and support you emotionally. They also continue to need your support and encouragement.

79TH YEAR (78-79)

Your seventy-ninth year is a time when you are called again to express your creativity. This is a year when you may actively step forward to teach or to share with others the insights you have gained through these last few years of reconciliation and detachment. As a self actualized person and a wisdom keeper, you are respected and appreciated by others. They continue to feel inspired by your example and look forward to hearing whatever you want to share with them. In addition to sharing with your peers, you may also reach out to mentor, teach or counsel the next generation of students and teachers.

80TH YEAR (79-80)

If you have not completed your healing and forgiveness work, your eightieth year is a year when you must take the time to do so, or risk the possibility of not finding peace and reconciliation before you leave the body.

Take time to forgive yourself for your mistakes and trespasses and to forgive others who have injured you. Understand that this world is a learning laboratory. You don't come into this world understanding how to love yourself or how to love others. That is something that you learn how to do.

Learning and forgiveness go hand in hand. If you hold onto your mistakes or the mistakes of others and continue to blame and shame each other, you will not learn the lessons you have come here to learn.

The truth is that all of us do the best we can with the consciousness that we have at the time. When your consciousness expands, you become capable of living with more understanding and compassion. All the events of your life—including those that were most challenging for you—have conspired to help you grow into a more spiritual and compassionate human being.

81 ST YEAR (80-81)

This is the last year of your ninth cycle. It is your quintessential nine year, the year of true completion. For the last nine years you have been detaching from the outer aspects of your life and moving into your core self. Now that process is coming to fulfillment. You are coming to God with empty hands and an open heart. You have made peace with yourself and with others. Your journey here is complete. Whether you live for many more years or die tomorrow, you can accept what happens without anxiety or resistance. You live in the place where life is ever-present and eternal, where the end meets the beginning, and alpha (0) and omega (9) are joined as one.

4

PART FOUR

Numerological Applications

DETERMINING YOUR SOUL VIBRATION

Your soul vibration is found by calculating the sum of the numerical values of the letters in the name that you were born with (full legal name). Each letter in your name has a numerical value. To find out the value of each letter, please refer to the table below.

1	2	3	4	5	6	7	8	9
a	b	c	d	e	f	g	h	i
j	k	l	m	n	o	p	q	r
s	t	u	v	w	x	y	z	

For example, Abraham is 1+2+9+1+8+1+4 = 26 and Lincoln is 3+9+5+3+6+3+5 = 34.

Then add together the values of all of the names you were born with. Look at your birth certificate if you are unsure of your full legal name. For example, Abraham Lincoln is 26+34 = 60. Then reduce it to a number between 1 and 9 by adding the digits of the numbers together. For example 60 is 6+0= 6. So the name Abraham Lincoln has a six vibration.

If you change your name later in life, you should also compute the numerological value that corresponds to the name you are now using, especially if you have used it for many years. People who marry and take on the spouse's surname or combine their surnames will be bringing in a new soul vibration.

WHAT IS YOUR SOUL VIBRATION?

The soul vibration is the number that represents the energy that you bring into this embodiment, as well as the area in which your talents and gifts manifest.

Your soul vibration tells you the primary energetic focus of your life. If your soul vibration is a two digit number between 1 and 81, you may want to look at that year in Part 3 of this book, as that year may have a special significance in your life.

DETERMINING YOUR LIFE PATH

Your life path is calculated by adding together the day, month and the year of your birth. First add the day and month values together. Then add the year values together. Then find the sum of both numbers. For example, Abraham Lincoln was born February 12, 1809. So February 12 would be 2+12 =14 and 1809 would be 18+9 = 27. The sum of the two 14+27 = 41.

If you obtain a two digit number, add the digits together to get a number between 1 and 9. For example 41 is 4+1= 5.

If your life path is a number between 1 and 81, you may want to look at the description of that year in Part 3, as it may be a significant year for you.

WHAT IS YOUR LIFE PATH?

Your life path is the area of life in which you experience your greatest challenges and your greatest growth. Your life path brings the lessons in your life and helps to build your character as a person.

AN EXAMPLE OF SOUL VIBRATION AND LIFE PATH

For example, Abraham Lincoln had a soul vibration of six. He brought his six qualities of compassion and the desire to serve others into the area of public service. In that arena, he sought to fulfill his need for acceptance and belonging, and for the public approval that often eluded him.

Lincoln's life path was a five. That means that most of the challenges and lessons of his life would have had to do with his need to individuate and think outside of the box and his consequent courage to stand up for what he believed in.

When you look at the six and the five together, you can see how his lessons in life forced Lincoln to make unpopular decisions. He chose to stand alone for principles that he believed in. That often prevented him from attaining the approval and acceptance he hungered for.

DETERMINING YOUR NUMEROLOGICAL SIGNATURE

Your numerological signature is obtained by adding the number that corresponds to your soul vibration to the number that corresponds to your life path. For example, Abraham Lincoln's numerological signature is a 2 (6 + 5 =11 and 1+1 = 2).

WHAT IS YOUR NUMEROLOGICAL SIGNATURE?

Your numerological signature indicates the synergy between your soul vibration and your life path. It is what you achieve in your life.

For example, exhibiting the dualism of the number 2 (his numerological signature) Lincoln was a figure who was loved and hated. His decisions pitted brother against brother, spilling more blood than had ever been spilled on American soil. Yet the result of his life was the emancipation of slaves and the end of slavery. With five being the love of freedom, and six being the desire for acceptance, harmony and community, it is clear that life forced Lincoln to make difficult choices that brought benefit to others, while intensifying his own suffering and transformation. In that sense, he exhibits some of the six qualities of the martyr who gives his life for the sake of others. In the end, we know Lincoln as a larger than life figure who helped our country achieve greater justice and freedom for all its citizens.

SKILLFUL PREPARATION

If you plan to use the concepts in this book to understand your soul vibration, life path and numerological signature, it is important that you master the meaning of the nine root numbers described in Part 2 of this book. Once you do that you will need to use your intuition to synthesize the meaning of the numbers and to connect the dots between these concepts and the major events and circumstances of your life. This is not a superficial undertaking.

Moreover, all symbolical systems, including this one, are meant to be tools that can help us better understand ourselves and others. They are not meant to be used in a rigid or narrow fashion. The idea is not to try to fit your life into the meaning of the numbers, but to allow your understanding of the numbers to shed light on the major themes and challenges of your life.

As in all quests for genuine understanding, an open heart and an open mind are essential. Neither analysis nor intuition by itself will help you to see the whole picture. Both are necessary.

POSTSCRIPT

I sincerely hope that you find this book helpful and that you will use it wisely to shed light on the cycles that are operating in your life. Moving with the current of the river is always more satisfying than trying to swim upstream against it.

There are times in life (years 3-7) when you need to be moving outward into the world with energy and enthusiasm. Those are not times to procrastinate or hold back.

On the other hand, there are other times when you need to turn within to find guidance and welcome new energy into your life (years 1-2), and times when you need to turn inward to find reconciliation and to detach from old energetic patterns (years 8-9). Those are not years when you should expect to be outwardly engaged and productive.

Because we are wounded and confused by life, we often swim against the tide, pushing ourselves to be active when we need to rest and go within, or holding ourselves back when it is time for us to participate fully in the world. This makes it hard for us to learn our lessons and to express our gifts.

Even if you just understand the basic concepts of the nine year cycle and the way each cycle unfolds within your overall life, you should be able to better attune to the energies within you that need to be nurtured and expressed. That means less conflict within and fewer struggles without.

Tuning in to your changing needs and cooperating with the universal energy as it is expressed around you leads to a life of grace and abundance.

May that life be yours, now and for all your years to come.

Blessings,

Paul Ferrini

Paul Ferrini is the author of over 40 books on love, healing and forgiveness. His unique blend of spirituality and psychology goes beyond self-help and recovery into the heart of healing. His conferences, retreats, and *Affinity Group Process* have helped thousands of people deepen their practice of forgiveness and open their hearts to the divine presence in themselves and others.

For more information on Paul Ferrini's work, visit his website at www.paulferrini.com. The website has many excerpts from Paul's books, as well as information on his workshops and retreats. Be sure to request Paul's email newsletter, his daily wisdom message, as well as a free catalog of his books and audio products. You can also email us at orders@heartwayspress.com or call us at 941-776-8001.

New Audio and Video by Paul Ferrini

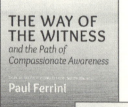

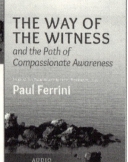

Available as a CD or DVD set

The Way of the Witness
and the Path of Compassionate Awareness

BY PAUL FERRINI

3 DVD set or 6 CD Audio set
with 5.5 hours of talks
Either set available for
$55.00.
ISBN # 978-1-879159-95-2

Talk #1 The Art of Bullfighting

Talk #2 The Way of the Witness:

Talk #3 Choosing Love

Talk #4 Being Yourself and Allowing Others to be Themselves

Talk #5 Giving up the Caretaker Role and Asking for what You Need

Talk #6 Two Powerful Triangles within the 8 Keys to the Kingdom

Available as a CD or DVD set

Healing Your Life
12 Steps to Psychologial and Spiritual
Transformation
BY PAUL FERRINI
$111.00   approxImately 11 hours
978-1-879159-93-8   www.paulferrini.com

In this powerful series of recordings, Paul Ferrini teaches his ground-breaking Roadmap to Spiritual Transformation. Paul developed this curriculum to help us move through our pain, heal our childhood wounds and step into our power and purpose in this lifetime. He describes in detail the 12 steps that take us out of denial into a process of deep psychological healing in which our masks are taken off, our patterns of self-betrayal are ended, and we begin to move through the Dark night of the Soul that ensues when the False Self begins to fall apart. The process is complete when the False Self dies and the light of the True Self is born within our consciousness and experience. Then, like a brightly colored butterfly, we leave our caterpillar-like self behind, spread our wings and begin to fly. The result is Self-Actualization on all levels.

New Books by Paul Ferrini

The Long-Awaited Roadmap to Self-Healing and Empowerment

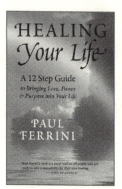

Healing Your Life
12 Steps to Heal Your Childhood Wounds
and Bring Love, Power & Purpose
into Your Life

BY PAUL FERRINI
ISBN: 978-1-879159-85-3
176 Pages   Paperback $14.95

Paul Ferrini finally shares his powerful 12-Step Roadmap to healing and transformation. This work is the fruit of 35 years of writing and teaching experience.

This book will help you open up to a life of genuine healing and empowerment. You can learn to love yourself from the inside out, initiating a process of giving and receiving that will transform your life. You can end your suffering and connect with your joy. You can find your passion in life and learn to nurture and express your gifts. You can learn to be the bringer of love to your own experience and attract more and more love into your life. You can fulfill your life purpose and live with your partner in an equal, mutually empowered relationship. All the gifts of life and love are possible for you. You need only do your part and open your heart to receive them.

"35 years of heart-centered spiritual work have taught me what is necessary to bring about a real, lasting change in a person's consciousness and experience."

— PAUL FERRINI

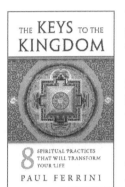

The Keys to the Kingdom
8 Spiritual Practices that will Transform Your Life

BY PAUL FERRINI
ISBN: 978-1-879159-84-6
128 Pages   Paperback $12.95

8 SPIRITUAL PRACTICES THAT WILL TRANSFORM YOUR LIFE

1. *Love Yourself*
2. *Be Yourself*
3. *Be Responsible*
4. *Be Honest*
5. *Walk Your Talk*
6. *Follow Your Heart*
7. *Be at Peace*
8. *Stay Present*

Please use the keys in this book to open the doorways in your life. Take the keys with you wherever you go. Use them as often as you can. They will help you to transform your experience. Fear will drop away and unconditional love will shine through. As you awaken to who you are, so will the people around you.

A fearful world cannot exist for a loving heart. Love changes everything. That is why this works. Do your part, and you will see for yourself.

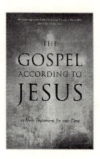
If you know me in your heart, you embody my teaching with an inner certainty. You know that love is the only answer to your problems.

When you give love you cannot help but receive it. Indeed, the more you give, the more you receive. There is no deficiency of love in the world. Love lives in the heart of every human being. If it is trusted, it has the power to uplift consciousness and change the conditions under which you live.

Love is the ultimate reality. It is the beginning and the end, the alpha and the omega. It emanates from itself, expresses itself and rests in itself. Whether rising or falling, waxing or waning, ebbing or flowing, it never loses touch with what it is.

I may not be present here in a body, but I am present in your love. When you find the love in your heart, you know that I am with you. It is that simple.

The long-awaited sequel to *Dancing with the Beloved*

When Love Comes as a Gift
Meeting the Soul Mate in this Life

BY PAUL FERRINI
ISBN: 978-1-879159-81-5
176 Pages Paperback $12.95
ebook $10.00

The soul mate is not just one person, but a work in progress, a tapestry being woven out of light and shadow, hope and fear. Every lover we have prepares us to meet the Beloved. Each one brings a lesson and a gift and each defers to another who brings a deeper gift and a more compelling lesson.

Our partner challenges us to become authentic and emotionally present. S/he invites us to walk through our fears, to tell the truth and to trust more deeply. Gradually, we open our hearts to the potential of creating intimacy on all levels.

And then it is no longer a temporal affair. It is Spirit come to flesh. It is the indwelling Presence of Love, blessing us and lifting us up. It is both a gift and a responsibility, both a promise made and a promise fulfilled.

Recent Workshop and Retreat Recordings

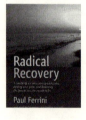

Radical Recovery

A Roadmap for overcoming addictions, healing your pain, and becoming the person you are meant to be

ISBN for CD Set 978-1-879159-91-4
Available as a 2 CD Set for $24.95
or as 2 Audio Downloads for $19.99

Resurrecting our Pain into Light

Healing our Trauma, Overcoming our Guilt and Taking ourselves off the Cross

ISBN for CD Set 978-1-879159-92-1
Available as a 5 CD Set for $55
or as 5 Audio Downloads for $49

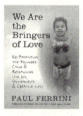

We are the Bringers of Love

Re-Parenting the Wounded Child
& Reclaiming Our Joy, Spontaneity and Creativity

ISBN for CD Set 978-1-879159-90-7
Available as a 4 CD Set for $44
or as 5 Audio Downloads for $41

Freedom from Self-Betrayal

Spiritual Mastery Talks at Palm Island
ISBN 978-1-879159-87-7
6 CDs $59.95

Putting Flesh on the Bones

Recordings from the 2009 Retreat in Santa Fe, New Mexico
5 CDs $49.00   ISBN 978-1-879159-80-8

Audio by Paul Ferrini

Real Happiness
Awakening To Our True Self
An Introductory Talk by Paul Ferrini
1 CD $16.95   ISBN 978-1-879159-75-4

Roadmap to Real Happiness
Living the Life of Joy and Purpose
You Were Meant to Live
Part 1 4 CDs $48.00
ISBN 978-1-879159-72-3
Part 2 3 CDs $36.00
ISBN 978-1-879159-73-0

Creating a Life of Fulfillment
Insights on Work, Relationship and Life Purpose
2 CDs $24.95
ISBN 978-1-879159-76-1

Being an Instrument of Love
in Times of Planetary Crisis
Two Talks on Individual and Collective Healing
2 CDs $24.95   ISBN 978-1-879159-79-2

The Radiant Light Within
Readings by Paul Ferrini from the *Hidden
Jewel* & *Dancing with the Beloved*
1 CD $16.95   ISBN 978-1-879159-74-7

Made in United States
Troutdale, OR
07/28/2024

21603036R00128